AF428424

politics. *One Betrayal Too Many* highlights the courage it took for Rich to leave MAGA and serves as a blueprint for those in MAGA who can no longer justify the lies of Donald Trump.

Joe Walsh, Former United States Representative

In *One Betrayal Too Many*, Rich Logis courageously confronts the pervasive disinformation and radicalism that have infiltrated our political landscape, particularly within the MAGA movement. As a former Republican Congressman and the technical director of the January 6th Select Committee, I have witnessed firsthand the devastating impact of lies and conspiracy theories on our democracy.

Logis' journey from the clutches of disinformation and misinformation to a commitment to truth mirrors my own struggle against the whitewashing of January 6 and the narratives that seek to distort our reality. His insights illuminate the dangers of radicalism and the urgent need for a return to factual discourse.

This book is not just a personal reflection; it's a vital call to arms for those of us who believe in the integrity of our democratic institutions. Rich's transformation serves as a beacon of hope, reminding us that it's never too late to embrace sanity over delusion. *One Betrayal Too Many* is essential reading for anyone who wishes to understand the dangers of our current political environment and the price of silence in the face of disinformation. I wholeheartedly endorse this powerful testament to truth, resilience, courage, and the unwavering fight for democracy.

Denver Riggleman, Former United States Representative

Rich's contributions to the *MeidasTouch Network* have been invaluable. *One Betrayal Too Many* is an optimistic work that speaks to the power of changing one's mind when confronted by truth. Our democracy will be stronger thanks to Rich's insights.

Ben Meiselas, Co-Founder, *MeidasTouch Network*

Rich Logis knows MAGA from the inside. His book is a drama of seduction and awakening. It's also an education for the rest of us about this movement that is now at the center of American politics.

William Kristol, Editor at Large, *The Bulwark*

Many of us wonder whether taking back our country to some semblance of the rule of law and sanity is really possible. Rich Logis's story gives me hope. Winning elections is paramount, but not enough. Saving our democracy will also require that we work to change the hearts and minds of people easily swayed by the message of a demagogue and his followers. Rich's searing account of his MAGA years and his courageous escape is a must read if we are to reclaim the best of American values.

Darrell Steinberg, former Democratic California State Senate Leader and Mayor of Sacramento

As someone who spent years as a Republican operative, I understand how hard it is to walk away from a movement that defines your identity, community, and sense of purpose. Rich's account of his journey out of MAGA is thoughtful, courageous, and deeply patriotic. This book is an essential read for anyone who believes introspection and personal accountability are strengths—not weaknesses—in our democracy.

Miles Bruner, former GOP Operative,
Founder, Breaking Ranks

If you want to understand how good people are seduced to go all in on anti-democratic movements—and, more importantly, how they find their way back out—*One Betrayal Too Many* is for you.

What makes Rich Logis' story so compelling is not outrage, but recognition. He doesn't begin as a caricature or a villain. He begins where you and I might, and millions did: drawn to a righteous outsider who promised to "drain the swamp" and stand up for people who felt ignored and disrespected. Step by step, Logis walks the reader down the same path he followed—from hopeful supporter, to fierce apologist, to podcaster idolized by his fans.

Then comes the reckoning. With rare honesty, Logis describes a long, lonely year in the metaphorical desert—after the slogans stopped working and the justifications collapsed. This is not a story of sudden awakening. It is a story of disorientation, grief, and moral courage.

While Logis writes from his own lived experience on the right, the lesson is broader. All of us—on the left and the right—can be seduced by a reality distorted and a lie denied, succumbing to our side's groupthink. Logis shows us how difficult—but necessary—it is to step back into the light.

I offer this recommendation as a lifelong Republican—often a contrarian one—who has spent years challenging my party to live up to its highest traditions, such as ending slavery and securing women's suffrage. Through Leaving MAGA, this journey now extends beyond memoir. It is an act of civic repair—revealing the emperor unclothed without mockery or contempt, and helping others reclaim their agency, their dignity, and their democratic responsibility.

One Betrayal Too Many doesn't tell readers what to think. It shows what it costs to tell the truth—and why, in the end, democracy depends on people willing to walk through the desert to find it.

Bill Shireman, Founder and President, Future 500

One Betrayal Too Many tells a hard truth our country can't afford to avoid. It names the damage MAGA has done and calls readers toward responsibility, courage, and the defense of democracy. Rich Logis know MAGA from the inside and names the real cost of staying silent. This book speaks directly to the urgency of this moment. It's a timely and necessary intervention for democracy.

Doug Pagitt, Pastor, Executive Director
Vote Common Good

Rich Logis has an important story to tell, and he tells it well here. I think he's made himself an important voice among a wave of Americans looking to find their way back to the values we all grew up embracing.

Billy Ray, American screenwriter (*Hunger Games,*
Captain Phillips) and film director
(*Shattered Glass, Breach*)

As someone with decades in the business of politics and consulting, I recognize the difference between the talkers and the doers. Rich is a doer; he understands well that action and empathy are the pathway to empowering others to leave MAGA. *One Betrayal Too Many* validates the work Rich continues to tirelessly do.

Reed Galen, President, Join The Union

Rich Logis' story of betrayal is strikingly similar to my own experience as a former member of the GOP. As an Alabama business owner, I regret my vote for Trump and am now running as a Democrat for the U.S. Senate, to help turn our country around. If you see the American Dream slipping away, *One Betrayal Too Many* will restore your faith in American democracy as we expose the falsehoods of the MAGA movement.

Kyle Sweetser, Candidate for U.S. Senate in Alabama

As an active supporter of the Democratic Party in both Florida and California, I know firsthand how important it is that we unite for America's future. Daily, we watch the lies of MAGA undermine the future of our country. Rich Logis gives readers a clear understanding of how a person could be deceived by this movement, and to find the path to clarity. Logis calls us to unite for the cause of democracy. It's a moment where being an American is more important than any other disagreements we might have. If you know someone in MAGA, this is the book you need.

Bob Poe, Former Chair, Democratic Party of Florida

I've spent years fighting inequality and injustice in Florida and across the country as MAGA's tactics have destroyed lives and communities. Rich Logis understands firsthand how propaganda works because he once believed it. His work now is focused on dismantling those lies, challenging the machinery that spreads them, and leaving the light on for people who are actively unlearning the myths they embraced. At the same time, he is clear that walking away is not enough. Rich has taken responsibility for the harm he helped enable and is committed to repairing what he helped break. He knows how to turn grassroots energy into real power, and he is using that power to confront an authoritarian administration and defend democracy.

Nadine Smith, President and CEO, Color of Change

Rich's story is an important one in these times. He gives an insider's look into how we all walk through life hoping to make the world a better place, but then sometimes realize that we can't put our heads in the sand when it comes to our integrity. For anyone who has taken a path and then regretted it, Rich's book is an honest look at how we can change our hearts and repair relationships we have damaged along the way.

Kelly Carlin-McCall, Founder, Humans on the Verge

Rich Logis' *One Betrayal Too Many* is a work of profound and courageous storytelling that serves as a necessary mirror for all of us. His journey from a seven-year MAGA activist to a dedicated defender of democracy reminds us of who we are as Americans and the importance of our shared values.

I am excited that his story is being told, alongside the many others he is now empowering through the Leaving MAGA community. It is individuals like Rich—who choose truth over dogma and accountability over silence—who will guide us out of the wilderness and toward a future of healing and reconciliation.

Austin Weatherford, President, Bright America

Rich Logis' transformational journey from a diehard MAGA adherent to a thoughtful, engaged American citizen is compelling. His slide into MAGA/Trumpworld is a cautionary tale of how easy it is for movements to demand our absolute allegiance, even as we believe ourselves to be independent thinkers. The human need for social connection is strong, and in our increasingly isolated, internet-oriented society, groups like MAGA seize upon that need. Rich's capacity to listen to his doubts and rising cognitive dissonance moved him to take the courageous leap to change his mind and actions. Rich's work in establishing Leaving MAGA has provided an exit ramp for those ready to leave and a community where amends are made for the harm done and healing is happening.

The Rev. Anjel Scarborough, Rector
All Saints Episcopal Church, Hershey, Pennsylvania

By Rich Logis' own account, life inside MAGA became a kind of hell marked by fear, deception, and chronic grievance. Many inside the MAGA world are exhausted, disillusioned, or quietly aware that something has gone wrong— but don't know how to leave without losing their community.

Rich Logis lived in that bubble too long, but found his way out through spiritual courage and moral reckoning. *One Betrayal Too Many* is not a judgment piece; rather, this book shows others that leaving MAGA is possible—and that a larger, healthier community awaits.

Michael J. Christensen, PhD, Professor of Theology, Northwind Seminary and Author, *C.S. Lewis on Scripture*

Far too many anti-Trump activists speak in insulting and condescending ways to and about their opponents. Ironically, this ends up creating more support for Trump. I respect Rich Logis for his commitment to treating his opponents with respect: to seeing the best in them, while also trying to change their minds. His past as a gung-ho Trump supporter gives him a valuable vantage point for understanding how to change minds. If we had more activists like Rich Logis (on either "side"), our politics would be less toxic and our country would be more functional.

Zach Elwood, Author
How Contempt Destroys Democracy

When I first met Rich, I was suspicious. He is a white man from Florida who once proudly dined at Mar-a-Lago and even defended MAGA after the January 6, 2021, insurrection. I am a Black man from Alabama who was the lead plaintiff in Allen v. Milligan, the litigation that successfully challenged racial vote dilution in our state's congressional redistricting and secured a second Black-opportunity district.

I wasn't sure if Rich was prepared for the negativity he would experience if Leaving MAGA achieved the vision he now outlines in *One Betrayal Too Many*. After observing him for a few years, I've become convinced that Rich and the Leaving MAGA network will achieve their vision and are prepared for the stakes of their journey. And because they are fueled by relentless commitment to building redemptive space, their victories will benefit millions of Americans who have felt afraid to request or offer forgiveness—most importantly for and to ourselves. This book challenges me to become more hopeful. I hope you will sit with it too.

Evan Milligan, Co-Director
The Sanctuary at Jubilee Community Center

Someone once asked Mother Teresa why she didn't participate in anti-war demonstrations. "I will never do that," she said, "but as soon as you have a pro-peace rally, I'll be there." This book is a pro-peace rally based on Rich Logis' desire to create community for those who are leaving MAGA. We can't simply cry, "peace, peace" when there is none; it is necessary to sit and listen to one another's stories. Reading this book has brought me a level of respect and compassion I did not expect, but desperately needed.

Janyne McConnaughey, PhD, Author, *Trauma in the Pews: The Impact on Faith and Spiritual Practices*

It's understandable and totally reasonable that one might encounter Rich Logis's political and spiritual conversion with a healthy degree of skepticism. But it's hard to dismiss his honesty and conviction, especially at a time when so few people are incapable of admitting they're wrong, and almost never publicly. A lot of people like to speculate about the MAGA movement—its rise or potential demise, but *One Betrayal Too Many* provides an authentic perspective from the inside, and just might point the way to a hopeful future.

Adam Howard, Senior Producer
The New Yorker Radio Hour

One Betrayal Too Many is not a redemption story. It is a field guide for leaving. Leaving a movement that replaces truth with loyalty and turns rage into belonging. Rich Logis understands that people do not exit extremism through shaming or debunking, but through honest reckoning and the presence of a real off-ramp. This book pairs accountability with something far rarer: a credible path back into community. Rich's work is grounded in lived experience, earned trust, and a sustained commitment to helping people leave without losing themselves.

Noelle Cook, Author, *The Conspiracists*

Rich Logis' *One Betrayal Too Many* is not only a gripping personal testimony, but a vital contribution to one of the most urgent challenges of our time—ideological extremism and democratic backsliding. Told with courage and unflinching honesty, his story offers both a rare window into the psychology of radicalization and a powerful roadmap for healing and reintegration.

Rich brings a uniquely essential perspective: a firsthand account from within the MAGA movement—what draws people in, what holds them there, and what ultimately enables them to leave. Through Leaving MAGA, he's building a refuge of accountability, connection, and democratic renewal for those seeking a way out of extremism.

This book is more than a memoir—it's a critical tool for anyone committed to bridging divides, restoring trust, and building a truly inclusive democracy. Rich reminds us that redemption is possible, that listening is transformative, and that America's future remains both a warning and a promise.

Adrienne Evans, Executive Director
United Vision for Idaho

Don't give up on your MAGA friends. I know it can be frustrating having friends in a MAGA information bubble, unwilling to accept the role they are playing in the destruction of our democratic norms. Rich Logis' story shows that even some of the most diehard MAGA supporters have their breaking points. It may even come when we least expect it. *One Betrayal Too Many* shows not only how that can happen but how we, friends and family of MAGA supporters, should respond. If we get this right, we might even save our democracy.

Napp Nazworth, Executive Director, American Values
Coalition

The painstaking work of listening to one's conscience, of owning up to one's mistakes with humility, of placing the values of citizenship and commitment to democratic society above personal fame and gain—these are qualities Rich Logis embodies with integrity and sincerity. This memoir is a "conversion story," of someone who comes face to face with how he has been blinded by a political movement steeped in lies. In the end, virtue wins and Rich's story can help show a liberating pathway to those who feel duped and deceived by any oppressive cult or ideology.

Carl Procario-Foley, PhD, Executive Director and Adjunct Faculty, Iona University Center at Mariandale

When I first met Rich, his passion and focus were abundantly clear. To see Leaving MAGA's remarkable growth in just a few short years makes me proud to call him a friend and fellow defender of democracy. *One Betrayal Too Many* is a remarkable and candid work that generations of Americans will learn from.

Lia Gaines, Past President, West Palm Beach NAACP

I have known Rich since before Leaving MAGA was formed and have been closely following his progress. I evaluate founders through the lens of problem-founder-fit, and Rich is obsessed with solving how to loosen MAGA's undue grip on his fellow Americans. His scrappiness and will are among the most impressive I have ever encountered. *One Betrayal Too Many* offers a glimpse into Rich's founder journey, and his determination to help those caught in the thrall of MAGA escape.

Christopher Deutsch, Founder, Lofty Ventures

One Betrayal Too Many

WHY I LEFT MAGA

Many

RICH LOGIS

Founder of Leaving MAGA

One Betrayal Too Many: Why I Left MAGA
Copyright © 2026 Rich Logis

First paperback edition February 2026
Cover Design by: Kay McConnaughey
Interior Design: Carolyn Rafferty
Published by Writers Integrity Network
Glendora, California
writersintegritynetwork.com
ISBN: 979-8-9987743-6-2 (Hardback)
ISBN: 979-8-9987743-5-5 (Paperback)

CONTENTS

Adam Kinzinger

One day in January 2024, I was scrolling through Twitter when I came across something that snapped me to attention: Rich Logis, a man who had spent years ardently backing MAGA as an activist, writer, and podcaster, had publicly broken from the movement, and was apologizing for the harm he had done to the nation by spreading MAGA's lies and distortions.

I retweeted the post and encouraged people to follow Rich. He then reached out to me, and we've been friends ever since. He jokes that he hated me with a passion when he was in MAGA.

Rich's story resonated with me because of my own experience fighting to defend our constitutional democracy, and because his journey highlights one of the most challenging, critical tasks facing us: reaching out with compassion and empathy to the millions of people in MAGA.

I understand why so many Americans reject this way of thinking. After all the vilification I endured for voting to impeach Donald Trump and serving on the January 6 committee—decisions that destroyed my political career — I still get angry at times. When that happens, I remind myself that the people in

MAGA are human beings, and that they think they're doing what's best for the country.

My political career began in the cockpit. As an Air Force pilot, I flew dozens of air refueling, surveillance, and reconnaissance missions over Iraq and Afghanistan. While I was flying a mission one day, it occurred to me that if I was willing to fight for my country overseas, I should also be willing to fight for it at home.

My patriotic aspirations quickly ran into a disturbing reality. Early on in my congressional career, I discovered a discouraging trend: toxic tribalism. Politics had become more like a sport. Winning became more important than governing, and our opponents became our enemies.

Instead of just disagreeing with our political adversaries, we dehumanized them. Too many of my colleagues became more focused on performing for cable news than on governing. I admit to being complicit in this process; I went along with it.

This debasement of our politics culminated with the Jan. 6, 2021, attempt to block the peaceful transfer of power, the first time this had happened in the history of the republic. Trump's attempted coup changed me forever. No longer would I be the loyal party member who ignored or explained away the excesses of its leader.

I was one of ten House Republicans who voted to impeach Trump for his perfidy. And I proudly served as one of the two Republican members of the Select Committee that investigated January 6. Predictably, the GOP ostracized me. The threats poured in. Several relatives disowned me. It all took a terrible toll on my family and me. Despite all of that, I knew I was on the right side of history—I was defending the truth.

> *Trump's attempted coup changed me forever. No longer would I be the loyal party member who ignored or explained away the excesses of its leader*

Embracing the truth—having common agreement on what is reality—is a critical aspect of the fight to save our democracy. When Trump and his MAGA enablers knowingly lie to advance their agenda, they are undermining the very foundations of our republic.

The Founders came up with the brilliant idea of creating a country based on checks and balances among three coequal branches of government. Until Donald Trump came along, that infrastructure seemed impregnable. Today, it's cracking and straining in the face of his authoritarian onslaught.

Those of us who love our democracy must fight back on all fronts. But we can never win this war if we fail to recognize the humanity in our opponents. We can't fall prey to the same sort of toxic tribalism that transformed the GOP into a party of Trump sycophants.

And that's where Rich Logis and Leaving MAGA come in. Rich tells the tale of his odyssey with great honesty, forthrightness, and most importantly, humility. He understands how important community is to the people in MAGA, because he lived it. He appreciates that many in the movement are motivated by a love of country, because he was one of them. And he knows that browbeating, berating, or belittling people for their political choices will only make them more defensive about them.

> " Those of us who love our Democracy must fight back on all fronts. But we can never win this war if we fail to recognize the humanity in our opponents. We can't fall prey to the same sort of toxic tribalism that transformed the GOP into a party of Trump sycophants.

Through the Leaving MAGA nonprofit he formed, Rich has created a safe, nonjudgmental space for people who may be having doubts and questioning their support of Donald Trump.

The next chapter of American history is yet to be written. It's in our hands. I, for one, refuse to be part of the generation that lets our democracy fail, especially after my grandfather stared down the Nazis, and especially after my friends and I stared down Al-Qaeda. And I'm honored to have Rich Logis as an ally in this fight.

INTRODUCTION
An Apology and An Appeal

This book is a public apology. I am profoundly sorry for the damage I caused during the seven years I was in the MAGA movement. I contributed to the assault on our democracy. I exacerbated the harm caused to others in MAGA. Now I am holding myself accountable by working to make amends.

———◆———

As a former MAGA insider, I know people don't join for malicious reasons. The movement appealed to me because I felt unheard and disrespected by the political dysfunction in Washington, DC. I thought aligning myself with MAGA was a way to do something good and moral for my country. It gave me a sense of belonging to a community that shared common goals.

But it didn't take long before the relentless messages of fear, anger, and hatred changed me. If you had met me between 2015 and 2022, you wouldn't have recognized me as the same person I am today. MAGA brought out the worst in me. I distrusted anyone outside the movement. I pulled away from my previous friends and isolated myself on every level. I became Rich Logis, MAGA podcaster, extreme devotee of Donald Trump and his Make America Great Again message. I *became* MAGA.

Living in the MAGA echo chamber, I fully believed in Trump, even though time and again he promised one thing and delivered the opposite. Trump told one lie after another and I excused him. He villainized people and I looked the other way. I was swept up in a deception devised to undermine our democracy. MAGA betrayed me—not only politically, but morally as well. I didn't want to face it, but eventually my conscience became deeply troubled.

At the height of my struggle—what I call my "Year of Heaven and Hell"—I agonized between my growing doubts and my fear of losing everything I had built within the MAGA community. On top of that, it was simply hard to admit I was wrong. After many months of inner turmoil, there was one betrayal too many. In the spring of 2022, I finally faced the fact that I had been deceived. I knew I had to leave.

———◆———

Once free of MAGA, I resolved to dedicate myself to helping others find their way out. But to succeed, I needed a new community. When I couldn't find one, I started my own and named it Leaving MAGA. In 2024, it formally became a nonprofit organization. I am amazed by the growing number of former MAGA followers who have joined us. I've included some of their testimonials. Like me, they chose integrity and truth over fear and disinformation. Their accounts are honest, vulnerable and courageous.

Our stories are a wake-up call for those still in MAGA—especially those feeling betrayed by the movement's direction. If you are a MAGA follower and are now experiencing doubts, if you're questioning your decision, if you suspect that you've been lied to—this book is for you.

We are aware that the thought of leaving MAGA comes with the risk of losing your community. Leaving isn't just ideological; it's relational. We offer our stories to show you that it is possible to leave. There is life after MAGA.

———◆———

Neither the Leaving MAGA organization nor I advocate for a particular partisan outlook. One of our priorities is to provide people the freedom to find their own path. Their journey out of MAGA can lead them down a variety of roads; our members are conservative, moderate, and progressive. They hold their own views on the issues of the day, and they certainly differ with one another at times.

That said, Americans agree much more than we disagree. The vast majority of us want to live in a constitutional republic, not under authoritarianism. The one value we hold in common at Leaving MAGA is this: *MAGA is antithetical to democracy.* And MAGA's insistence on groupthink stands in stark contrast to Leaving MAGA's ethos of restoring personal agency and intellectual dignity.

———◆———

To those of you who can't comprehend why anyone would be tempted to throw their lot in with MAGA, I hope my odyssey brings you a greater measure of understanding. I'm painfully aware that millions of relationships have suffered because of angry disagreements about Trump or MAGA. This book offers MAGA's critics an opportunity to understand how difficult it is to leave.

When it comes to your family or friends who have quit the movement, you have a significant role to play. Will you create a pathway toward healing and reconciliation, or will you perpetuate division? Lost relationships can be reclaimed if you emphasize compassion rather than ideological point-scoring. Ultimately, our country can heal only if we come together.

Trump and MAGA have tried to redefine our vocabulary. True patriots have been called terrorists while those trying to undermine democracy are labeled as the "real" Americans. We must lay claim to our rightful place as Americans, united in defense of democracy and in pursuit of liberty and justice for all.

Here are my personal declarations:

- Because I am an American, I believe in our bedrock constitutional values and freedoms.
- Because I am an American, I recognize the grave threats posed by MAGA.
- Because I am an American, I refuse to cower in fear or abdicate my duties as a citizen.

Because I believe in Americans, I know that our country's best days can be ahead of us. But we must be willing to do what is necessary to see America through our current moment of darkness and despair.

Because you are an American, you have a choice.

PROLOGUE
The Amazing Mar-a-Lago
October 29, 2020

Even knowing that President Trump wouldn't be here, I still couldn't help but feel electrified while driving up the gravel driveway onto the manicured grounds of Mar-a-Lago. It was October 29, not long before the 2020 election. It felt like I was a part of all the luxury and opportunity that surrounded me.

As the valet took my car, I stood on the sidewalk for a moment to take it all in. Dressed in a white tuxedo, at 6' 3", I gave off a Great Gatsby vibe. I'd studied the layout ahead of time so I would be able to walk through the rooms with confidence. The fact was, I'd never been there before, and it cost me a small fortune to rub shoulders with those who were attending the annual ball. Taking a deep breath, I congratulated myself. "Rich, you are actually *here*."

I could honestly say that there was not a more devoted Trump supporter. I'd invested everything—my money, time, and energy. As Rich Logis, MAGA podcaster, writer, and activist, I'd gathered regional notoriety and even had followers across the country. I was there to hobnob my way up the ladder, knowing that national leaders would be in attendance. It would all be worth it when I gained the president's attention and was recognized as a loyal MAGA soldier.

When I arrived at the entrance, I felt exhilarated. I moved through an elegantly dressed crowd into an expansively ostentatious den. The high ceilings above me were filled with resplendent chandeliers and rich, dark wood paneling covered the walls around me.

> " I could honestly say that there was not a more devoted Trump supporter. I'd invested everything —my money, time, and energy.

I made my way through the den and out onto the back patio overlooking a pool. Tuxedoed servers moved through the crowd, serving drinks and offering choices from large platters of finger foods.

I looked around for my friends and fellow Trump supporters. We figured we would fill up about three tables, but we knew we had to enter the banquet at the same time to make that happen. I didn't want to be left behind — not tonight, of all nights.

Snagging a drink, I kept surveying the happy, bustling crowd—everyone looked as excited as I was to be there. In the distance, the sun was descending over the ocean, its reflection casting a narrow orange glow between the lush greenery and the deep ocean-blue sky. Lights flickered on around the pool and across the complex, perfectly highlighting the splendor of the buildings and the foliage.

"Hey, Rich!" I heard a man's voice as Andy emerged from the throng. "I'm glad to see you!" Andy and I had been part of the local Trump network in Fort Lauderdale, Florida.

We shook hands. "Great to see you! And you, Lisa!" I said, turning to his wife.

"I'm so glad to meet you, finally!" Lisa smiled. Then, in a voice meant to mimic my show's announcer, she added, "I listen to your podcast all the time!"

Hearing Lisa's parody of my podcast lead-in, a man walking by stopped and asked, "Are you Rich Logis? Of the podcast?"

I nodded. He grabbed my hand and gave me a slap on the back. "Rich, you are a bit of a legend around here, you know."

This was heaven, as far as I was concerned. Maybe my dream would come true and those higher up in the organization would notice me. With this kind of support, it was possible.

————◆————

The room was abuzz with conversation when the doors of the ballroom opened, indicating it was time to be seated. Our group joined approximately 300 other enthusiastic supporters filing into the massive main ballroom that provided the perfect mix of celebration and opulence. VIPs and special guests entered through a separate entrance and I strained my neck to see who might be arriving on the red carpet.

The tables were covered in starched white tablecloths with formal settings of bone China, cutlery, and glassware that sparkled with reflected light from the chandeliers overhead. At the other end of the room was a large stage, filled with balloons and flower arrangements, surrounding a podium. Soft music played from the overhead speaker, while excited voices enthusiastically greeted each other and lights flashed as phones took videos and photographs.

Our group entered together, quickly found three adjacent tables, and took our seats. We marveled over the extravagant decor while giving our meal choices to the servers. Several of us took advantage of the open bar, returning to our tables just as our salads were delivered. As soon as the main entrée was served, the program began with customary announcements and introductions of dignitaries.

The room came alive with applause when Tucker Carlson took the stage. As he spoke, we were more than willing to be stirred into a wildly cheering crowd at the prospect of a second Trump victory. He garnered the desired boos and groans at the mention of Joe Biden. His remarks ended with enthusiastic applause and he left the stage a conquering hero.

Kristi Noem, the evening's keynote speaker, strode to the podium amid clapping and cheers. The crowd settled down to let her talk as someone yelled out, "Hey, Kristi! Are you single?" Her answer was lost amid a loud chorus of disapproving responses. Those of us at our table just looked at each other and rolled our eyes.

Noem didn't miss a beat. Her message was one of strength and optimism, delivered with an unwavering confidence that Trump would win a second term. As I listened, a flash of anxiety sped through me. In my heart, I wasn't sure. After getting into politics, I'd always been good at predicting the outcome of elections. I had my doubts, but I wanted to believe Noem was right.

Like everyone else there, I was networking like crazy. If those with influence knew my name, then maybe I'd rise in the ranks. Who knew? Maybe I'd be acknowledged as helping get Trump elected a second time. I was with my people, and I wanted them to be right about a second Trump administration. So I joined the chorus, declaring that 2020 would be an easy win.

———◆———

When the evening came to a close, the valet and I traded my keys for his tip. Guiding my car down the lit driveway to exit the complex, I marveled over the fact that I had just shared an evening in the company of such powerful and influential people. When I attended my first MAGA event back in 2016, I never imagined the unexpected turns my life would take over the past four years. I smiled to myself as I headed home with Mar-a-Lago in my rearview mirror.

> " I was with my people, and I wanted them to be right about a second Trump administration.

PART 1

Joining MAGA
From Alienated Independent to MAGA Winner

2016
Four Years Earlier

CHAPTER 1
Disappointed in Democracy

Running a bit late for an early afternoon gathering in February 2016, I quickly walked into the restaurant and looked around for signs of a meeting. Recognizing my lost look, the host asked, "Are you here for the Trump training?" I nodded and he directed me to a private meeting room.

At the end of the hall, I spotted a smiling Trump volunteer sitting at a small table in front of the meeting room entrance. She was wearing a red *Make America Great Again* T-shirt and a name tag that read "Marge." Leaning toward me, Marge whispered, "The meeting has already started, but you're welcome to join us." She eagerly handed me a printed flier, a name tag, and a marker.

I quickly filled out the name tag, and pinning it to my shirt, I stepped through the door. Not wanting to draw attention to myself, I slipped quietly into the back of the wood-paneled room and found my way to a nearby table, certain I wouldn't stay too long. I just wanted to check out this Trump phenomenon.

Fifty or so volunteers sat at long tables listening to the speaker who, according to the flier I'd just been given, was Madeline Masters, the head of Trump's effort in the area. Maddy, as people called her, was also wearing a red MAGA T-shirt. I smiled smugly as I noticed that most of the room was a sea of red shirts. I couldn't imagine myself being one of "those" people in matching outfits.

Half listening to the speaker with my arms crossed, I asked myself, *Why am I even here at this Trump thing?* I immediately knew the answer. We were approaching the 2016 election and I didn't like my choices.

To my mind, the political hand-offs between the Republican and Democratic parties had little impact—it appeared to be the same song with the same rotation of singers. In the span of fewer than three decades, we'd had three Bush administrations and two Clinton administrations. And now it seemed the nominees would be another Clinton (Hillary) and another Bush (Jeb).

I resented what I perceived as hubristic entitlement; neither Bush nor Clinton were owed their respective parties' nominations. The situation reinforced my belief that the Republicans and Democrats didn't play by the rules we plebes were obliged to follow. As I saw it, this was not just further proof of a "uniparty"—it meant the country was becoming a quasi-monarchy.

Every election, I had voted third-party. Every election, my candidate lost, and I felt more alienated and angry. But the prospect of another Bush or Clinton in the White House drove my dissatisfaction with all things political to new heights.

Without realizing it, I lost faith in the democratic system itself. Where were the checks and balances promised to keep our country on track for the betterment of American citizens? How could these self-serving politicians get away with enriching themselves and not fight for the needs of their constituents? A deep cynicism smoldered under the surface.

> "In the span of fewer than three decades, we'd had three Bush administrations and two Clinton administrations. And now it seemed the nominees would be another Clinton (Hillary) and another Bush (Jeb).

How did I become so skeptical? Considering this question requires me to reflect back on my childhood.

———◆———

Born on January 30, 1977, in Westchester County, New York, I grew up in a quintessentially middle-class Catholic household: small house, big yard, two modest cars, kids in public school, and a lake in our community that we considered a second home.

My father worked a variety of jobs. He was an elevator inspector for the city of New York, delivered for Airborne Express, sold cars for a dealership, and was a field technician for a utility. My mother worked in the commercial insurance industry for decades; she also worked for a few years as a Walmart manager. Nothing out of the ordinary.

When I was five months old, Star Wars was released. As a kid, I became obsessed with the desire for a lightsaber so I could join Luke Skywalker and the Rebel Alliance in battle to defeat the evil Galactic Empire.

As far back as I can remember, my family never discussed politics. In fact, I have no recollection of my parents voting in any election. It was as if the outside world had no impact or significance whatsoever on our lives. The political reality wasn't simply ignored; for us, it did not exist.

Despite my family's lack of interest in politics, we lived in a turbulent time. I was born two years after the end of the Vietnam War, which had torn apart American society. When I was two, Iranian militants stormed the U.S. Embassy in Tehran and took 52 Americans hostage, sparking a 444-day standoff that helped Ronald Reagan defeat Jimmy Carter in the 1980 presidential election.

During my pre-teen years, the Iran-Contra scandal erupted. The ensuing congressional investigation described a "government organization operating outside the authority of Congress." The Reagan administration secretly sold weapons, including anti-tank missiles, to Iran in an effort to secure the release of U.S. hostages. Washington then diverted proceeds from the sales to buy weapons for the Contra rebels fighting Nicaragua's Cuban-backed government, circumventing a congressional ban on lethal aid. National Security Council

> *I have no recollection of my parents voting in any election. It was as if the outside world had no impact or significance whatsoever on our lives.*

staffer Oliver North admitted to altering and destroying key documents and lying to Congress. When my fifth grade teacher discussed the affair in class, I was distraught that the president was involved in illegal activities. How could I respect my own president?

The year I turned twelve was tumultuous. The world watched in amazement as the Berlin Wall fell, just two years after Reagan declared, "Mr. Gorbachev, tear down this wall!" The Chinese government slaughtered student protestors in Tiananmen Square. The United States invaded Panama, captured its leader Manuel Noriega, and transported him back to Florida to stand trial for drug trafficking.

None of these events personally affected me, or if there was an impact, I had no awareness. What was truly significant to me was our family's move from urban Yonkers, New York, to Shrub Oak, a bucolic hamlet in the town of Yorktown. Living in a house rather than being cooped up in a small apartment, I reveled in the freedom of growing up in suburban America—a grand adventure for a twelve-year-old boy.

I entered high school in 1992—the same year Bill Clinton won the election that began his eight-year presidency. I was an avid reader but didn't apply myself to my studies. Instead, I exercised my critical thinking skills by perusing left-of-center magazines like *The Progressive*, *The Nation*, and *The New Republic*.

My primary focus wasn't on Clinton or politics, but on a massive growth spurt that propelled me to my full adult height of 6'3" at the age of fifteen. I was coordinated enough to excel on the basketball court, which gave me a place of belonging in the high school jungle. After school and weekends, you could find me on nearby courts marking my territory.

I was a natural at the sport, and had many strengths—I could shoot layups, dribble and pass with either hand, had strong peripheral vision, and, if the defender gave me space, I could hit three-point shots. Winning was everything to me, because while I was playing, I was somebody. I'm not sure if I was more motivated to win or desperate not to suffer the humiliation of losing. But either way, I became highly competitive in everything I did—extremely so.

My confidence while playing basketball was strikingly different from how I felt about myself in any other context. Off the court, I was socially awkward—certainly less secure than I was with a basketball in my hands. I developed a psychological toggle switch between confidence and shyness.

Perhaps my lack of self-esteem grew out of my family's lack of communication. During my senior year of high school, my parents separated. While I struggled to deal with the most traumatic event of my life up to that time, my parents acted as if nothing had happened. I remember thinking that they must have felt *something*, but they never created the space to process their feelings or mine. That left the palpable tension between them to fester over the next few years. They ultimately divorced after I graduated from college.

------♦------

I entered Iona College (later Iona University) in 1996. It was founded in 1940 by the Congregation of Christian Brothers, who were inspired by the sixth-century Irish monk Saint Columba, a patron saint to New York's Irish working class. I chose English as my major and developed my writing skills by joining the college newspaper staff. I satisfied my love of reading by devouring Shakespeare.

This was also the same year the Democrats continued their dominance, with Bill Clinton winning his second term as president. Even though I leaned left, Clinton's success did not influence my political ideology. However, since the college atmosphere was naturally charged with political energy, I paid attention to politics for the first time.

I was offended by the Monica Lewinsky scandal—here was yet another president lacking integrity—and by the GOP's cynical grandstanding about the importance of moral character to achieve its political ends. Both parties tried to take the moral high ground about Clinton's affair when neither deserved to claim it, which further solidified my disdain for politics as usual.

Iona championed community service through the lens of Catholic social justice. I channeled my youthful passion on this front into a couple of different areas.

> *Both parties tried to take the moral high ground about Clinton's affair when neither deserved to claim it, which further solidified my disdain for politics as usual.*

I joined the school newspaper as a copy editor and wrote articles with the intention of uncovering the story-behind-the-story. Journalism gave me a legitimate place to hone my writing skills and contribute to the ongoing conversation at the college and in the surrounding community.

During my junior and senior years, I served as a student leader in Iona's Campus Mission & Ministry Program, directed by Dr. Carl Procario-Foley. Being accepted into this program put me at the center of campus life and opened doors to experiences I would not have otherwise enjoyed.

I moved into a three-story house on campus called the Montgomery House with four other student ministry leaders and a staff member. We shared the responsibilities of taking care of the house, and were required to put in a specific number of hours each week in service projects, all while keeping our grades up. Broadly speaking, the school had tasked us with being leaders who contributed positively to Campus Ministries.

Once a month, we loaded 25-30 student volunteers into school vans, drove into Manhattan, and shared food, clothing and conversation with unhoused people. I believe the most important thing we offered was our time listening to their stories and giving them the honor and respect they deserved.

During my senior year Spring break, I joined a service project operated out of an inner-city Chicago church. I tutored kids from a local school, learned about outreach programs for gang members in public housing projects, and helped care for the hungry and homeless.

Despite Carl's mentorship, I got myself into some trouble during the Week of the Peacemaker, a campus educational week highlighting ways to respond to injustice. The themes included honoring the fifty-year anniversary of the founding of the United Nations, along with its commitment to nonviolence and its concern for the hungry and homeless.

One of Iona's traditions was to publish a literary magazine featuring writings by students and professors. The magazine was published without the university realizing that some of the students had used "the F-word" in their articles. As soon as it was brought to the administration's attention, there was a frenzy to gather them all up, edit the material, and republish that issue.

I was young and naive, full of piss and vinegar, and took great offense at what the university had done by reprinting the magazine. My opportunity to express my displeasure came during the annual open mic event where students traditionally read poems or sang. As expected, the room was packed with students, parents, alumni, professors, the college president, community members—and the local press.

I'm an awful singer, but I proudly rattled my tambourine and loudly belted out John Lennon's *Working Class Hero*, to publicly protest the censorship. "The F-word" is included twice in the lyrics and I made sure to emphasize both in my performance. After I finished, a deafening silence filled the room. I left the stage rather quickly. Carl was not happy.

———◆———

It took no time to be called into Carl's office in the Campus Ministries building. It was modest, with walls covered in community service awards and bookshelves filled with trophies. I took one of the two chairs facing his wooden desk. He looked at me with a level of disapproval I'd never seen before. We'd had a positive relationship up until this point, and I admired his leadership.

Carl didn't attack me. He didn't impugn my integrity. He didn't chastise me for what I did. Instead, he said, "Rich, you have the right to free speech and to express yourself how you choose. I respect your opinion and your right to share it. However, at the same time, you hold a position of leadership given to you by the college with the trust that what you say will also bring respect to all of us who make up this community. Your words have consequences, and what you said did not uphold the values of this institution."

"It wasn't a good look?" I asked.

Carl smiled slightly. "That's correct, Rich. It wasn't a good look."

I wondered if I'd be kicked out of the program. Other student leaders who had fallen short of requirements had been asked to leave. I didn't want to leave.

Carl continued: "I request that you make a formal apology to the school for the song you sang."

Relieved, I agreed. We stood up and shook hands, and I left the office a little wiser for the experience. From that time forward, Carl and I developed an even stronger relationship. He was my mentor and I realized that I had a lot to learn as a leader, as a man, and as a human being.

I issued an apology saying I was sorry for my language. That was supposed to be the end of the matter. However, my apology spurred more conversation about the event, not less. It became the talk of the campus as well as the larger community. Some speculated that I had been coerced to apologize. It even attracted local media attention. The *New York Times* and CNN did stories about it. So much for Carl's attempt to nip this in the bud.

But I had held up my part of the bargain, and when I applied the following year for the program, I was accepted again. Carl was a true mentor to me, exactly what I needed at that point in my life. We kept in touch after graduation and became lifelong friends.

———◆———

In 2000, when I was about to graduate, Vice President Al Gore (Clinton's man) and Texas Gov. George W. Bush (yet another Bush) launched their respective presidential campaigns. I wasn't interested in either of them.

By that point, I tended to lean left on social issues such as abortion and gay marriage. Since I didn't own a gun and had no intention of buying one, I didn't think much about the Second Amendment. But the massive movement of manufacturing jobs overseas and subsequent unemployment concerned me. I was also wary of how the country seemed to become embroiled in one war after another. My involvement in service programs during college made me wonder why our leaders couldn't focus more on America.

My views on these social issues only intensified as I watched the campaign unfold. The Democrats and Republicans seemed like two sides of the same coin—wealthy people who took turns moving the country back and forth, but never forward. As far as I was concerned, neither party adequately reflected my views. I felt unrepresented and alienated from the democratic process and was angry about it.

Then one day at the school library, simple happenstance radically altered my political trajectory. While reading a newspaper, I stumbled upon a headline that grabbed my attention: *The 2000 Campaign: The Green Party; Vowing to Restore Confidence, Nader Joins Race.* While I wasn't particularly motivated by environmental issues, Nader offered me something I'd never considered before: a third option. He shared my view that the Republican and Democratic parties were virtually indistinguishable. Finally, a candidate who was expressing what I felt.

> The Democrats and Republicans seemed like two sides of the same coin—wealthy people who took turns moving the country back and forth, but never forward.

More than addressing specific policy issues, the idea of a third option felt like I had found my political home. Nader personified a movement that wanted to reform the system itself. It didn't take long for me to be fully in his corner. My outsider status became my identity and developed into a point of pride.

Thanks to a controversial vote recount in Florida and an even more controversial Supreme Court ruling, Bush won the election. Democrats blamed Nader for drawing votes away from Gore. I didn't care if that was true. The outcome was of no concern to me, since one party was no different from the other. When President Bush invaded Iraq in 2003, I felt vindicated in my decision to vote third-party. And who could say that the Democrats would have done anything differently? What I wanted was to see democracy in action in

America, representing our citizens and focusing on our needs. Capturing oil fields didn't seem like a mission worthy of placing American soldiers in harm's way.

I graduated from college firm in my belief that the two-party system guaranteed that nothing would change for the better in America, and that our politicians would continue to ignore the people's needs. Meanwhile, I needed to make a life for myself after school, so politics once again took a back seat.

> *Nader personified a movement that wanted to reform the system itself. It didn't take long for me to be fully in his corner. My outsider status became my identity and developed into a point of pride.*

My first job out of college was as a reporter for *The Patent Trader* newspaper in New York's Westchester County. From 2000 to 2004, I covered every part of local news, except for sports. I found my footing, gained more confidence, and got married in 2008.

I quickly learned that it's nearly impossible to be a journalist without pursuing interviews with people who would rather not talk to you. Similar to being in sales, where one hears "No!" more often than not, I had to toughen up or fail—and I didn't like failing.

I loved being a journalist, because I could speak up, chase down interviews, challenge sources, and altogether channel my inner cockiness. It surprised and delighted me.

A few years later, I transitioned to insurance and financial advising. I was good at this job and I felt a similar confidence I used to have when playing basketball as a teenager. That work unexpectedly provided an inside look at the devastation that was suffered through the 2008 recession. My clients lost their jobs, their homes, and their investments. Having an up close and personal vantage point on this suffering just intensified my resentment toward the government.

In 2012, I met the producers of an AM radio show in Philadelphia that was broadcast from the attic of a Polish-American center near the Liberty Bell. The show focused on manufacturing and small-business entrepreneurship. I never intended to become a political activist, but when the producers of the weekly "American Workers Radio" program invited me to be a guest, I jumped at the chance.

In several appearances in the run-up to the presidential election, I railed against our duopolistic political system that forced millions to lose their homes, their retirement savings, and their jobs. My direct approach quickly found favor with listeners, and the producers asked me to be a regular weekly panelist. This unexpected gig ended up lasting ten years!

I was ecstatic to have a platform that not only allowed me to hone my broadcasting skills, but let me vent my rage at the two-party system to anyone who was willing to listen.

CHAPTER 2
My First Step Into MAGA

On June 16, 2015, Donald Trump descended the escalator in Trump Tower. I had been neutral about him. Thanks to the New York tabloids, I was somewhat familiar with what he had been up to. But I'd never watched The Apprentice, so I had missed out on the general sense of awe he had created around himself and his name.

Trump intrigued me because he was enough of a rogue that I felt he was a kindred spirit. I played the rogue every week on the radio; Trump was doing much the same, but on a much bigger scale.

I knew that Trump had been a Democrat but switched horses. It was irritating that he affiliated with either party, because he could have made an ideal third-party candidate. But as I watched the other Republican candidates denounce Trump during the primaries and Democrats show how threatened they felt by his appeal, my fascination with him grew. I loved that Trump terrified both the Democrats and traditional Republicans.

My fascination with Trump brought me to that training surrounded by red T-shirts and MAGA hats. Given my disdain for both major parties, I had no intention of becoming a Republican. And yet, there was something that drew me in.

Sitting in that room filled with Trump devotees while an intelligent woman presented her training materials, I thought, "Rich, pay attention, or this will be a waste of your afternoon." I tuned into what the presenter was saying, but under my breath, I whispered, "Okay, Maddy—Ms. GOP, do your best to convince me to support this guy. I dare you to convince me to support a Republican."

Maddy's excellent oratorical skills and personal passion for Trump captivated me. She said we had to defeat the Democrats if we wanted to truly change American politics. When Maddy said Trump would "drain the swamp," she encapsulated my years of smoldering frustration. Her words resonated with something deep in my soul

I leaned forward. Here I was, thirty-nine years old, and it seemed as if I might have finally stumbled onto a movement that could empower me to *actually do something* about the state of the nation. Yes, I had been appearing on the radio show, but could Trump be the "third-party" option I'd been waiting for, even if his merch was red? This unconventional, boastful, and powerful man shared my frustration with an ineffective democracy corrupted by the two major parties. Could he be my candidate?

Maddy further emphasized that people like us had a significant role to play in making this necessary change happen. How? By volunteering to make phone calls to people all over the country. This wasn't just a local effort; it was national.

Once she plunged into the mechanics of making phone calls, I was mesmerized. I imagined that we would just call people up on our phones. But no, it was much more complicated than that. You had to log on to a special website, click a button, and the computer would dial the call for you. Everything was planned down to the most minute detail. All of this was new and novel—and appealing. None of the third-party campaigns I worked on had this level of organization or sophistication.

> *Here I was, thirty-nine years old, and it seemed as if I might have finally stumbled onto a movement that could empower me to actually do something about the state of the nation*

When we took a break, I got some iced tea from the beverage table along with some cookies and energy bars. A man around my age introduced himself as Gregory. We began chatting.

Gregory said, "We've got to keep those Democrats from turning this country into a socialistic state."

I agreed. I didn't support the Democrats at all. But then again, I didn't support the Republicans, either. But, not interested in picking a fight, I asked him why he took the time to come to the training.

He said, "I have a lot of respect for Trump's business expertise. He's not a politician. He's a businessman and that's what we need. Look at what's happened to the manufacturing sector. We need to put America first!"

That rang true to me. "Yes, we need to rebuild American manufacturing rather than send jobs overseas," I said.

Gregory responded, "And why are we constantly getting into these wars? Why do politicians see fit to involve us in every skirmish and war around the globe? Let's take care of ourselves."

I was about to agree when Maddy called us back to our seats. Gregory invited me to move up and sit by him. The next thing I realized the three-hour boot camp was finished and I was still sitting there. I hadn't expected to spend the entire afternoon at this meeting.

I said goodbye to Gregory and was about to leave when I thought I'd introduce myself to Maddy and tell her how impressed I was with her presentation. I told her I was a registered Independent and hadn't yet decided whom I would support in the election.

Maddy smiled and asked more questions, seeming to be genuinely interested in my background. I told her I had been a journalist and I had a background as a writer.

Maddy's smile grew. Reaching back on the table behind her, she picked up some papers stapled together and said, "We're working on the script that all of our volunteers will use when they make their phone calls. Would you be willing to take a look and make some contributions to it?"

I was flattered that she would entrust me to contribute to something as important as their official script. But I paused. *Did I want to volunteer any time to this thing?*

Then she said, "We could use your professional input,"

and handed me the papers. I surprised myself by taking them. As I walked away, I felt oddly excited about being asked to participate—and a bit confused by my uncharacteristic group-joining behavior.

———◆———

While I sat at the bar looking over the script, some of the volunteers came in and we started chatting. It was easy to talk with them because they were so upbeat and welcoming, like they were all part of something important. I was envious that they felt that way.

I decided to tell the group about how I interviewed Trump back in 2002, when I was a reporter for *The Patent Trader*.

Trump had wanted to build a private golf course in Yorktown, and critics had raised concerns about the pesticides and other chemicals needed to treat the course's grass. "A source tipped me off about something very few people knew," I said. "Trump wanted to use a public body of water for the course. My research led me to a golf course Trump owned in Palm Beach County, Florida. I learned that the course's annual water usage exceeded its municipally approved allotment by tens of thousands of gallons."

> " It was easy to talk with (the Trump volunteers) because they were so upbeat and welcoming, like they were all part of something important.

Everyone listened intently as I continued. "I contacted Trump to give him a chance to respond to the local opposition. He insisted he would do everything by the book and that the course would be among the finest in the world."

Several nodded; it did sound like Trump.

"I asked him, 'What about the water overuse at your Florida course?' He said, 'Almost every golf course overuses its allotment.'"

"Was that true?" one of the volunteers asked.

"From my research, I knew it was true, so I was satisfied with his answer. My article ran on the front page. The next day, our newsroom received a fax from the Trump Organization: Trump had decided to abandon his plans for the golf course. No reason was given. I was curious about his change of heart, so I called him again. I asked, 'What do you intend to do with the land? It's over 400 acres.'"

"Did he answer you?" another volunteer asked.

"He did. He said, 'Now, why would I tell you that?' I countered with, 'Because I asked.' He chuckled but didn't give me an answer."

The group chuckled too. Then, someone asked, "Do you think your article caused him to pull out of the deal?"

I shrugged. "I don't know. But my source told me later that the land was donated to the state of New York as the Donald J. Trump State Park."

The conversation continued until people began to head out. It was fun to share that story with folks who thought it was special to have actually talked to the man they so admired. It felt easy to be with them, as if we were already good friends. I hadn't planned to stay that day, but now I had a strong feeling I would return.

———◆———

While looking forward to the next training, I reflected on my grievances about the country's ongoing political gridlock. I identified three areas of greatest concern to me—all of which were based on trust, or more accurately, my distrust.

The first and perhaps most fundamental problem stemmed from my inability to know who to trust. I thought of that old joke: "How do you know when a politician is lying? When their lips are moving." The "spin" on events came from both parties, and it was next to impossible to know whose version of events was more accurate.

As biased cable shows masqueraded as serious journalism, I grew increasingly distressed over the lack of genuine standards that had guided me when I worked in that field. How could one find accurate information about world events? Who could be trusted? The left? The right? The middle? Was anyone truly objective?

The lack of trust led to my second concern: the disruptive role money played in shaping politics. I believed members of Congress from both sides of the aisle used their access to privileged information to line their pockets. There was no way to ensure our representatives acted with integrity in their dealings. I simply assumed that public servants would leave their positions in government richer than when they first arrived.

The role of big money in elections also distressed me. Regular Americans didn't have the same access to members of Congress as did lobbyists, large donors or those connected to powerful people. I stood outside this elite group, which intensified my sense of powerlessness.

My third concern arose from the growing divide among the American public. My frustration over not knowing whom to trust in the media, along with my distrust of government in general, fueled a disdain for Americans I saw as having been duped into trusting one party or the other. They seemed oblivious to the reality that both Democrats and Republicans were scamming them.

> " The role of big money in elections also distressed me. Regular Americans didn't have the same access to members of Congress as did lobbyists, large donors, or those connected to powerful people.

The more I thought about American politics, the angrier I became. There wasn't enough to salvage. I wanted to tear down Washington, DC and start over.

———◆———

The following month, I went to our second volunteer meeting. Maddy stood up front as people reported on their activities. It felt she had read my mind as she articulated my three grievances and showed how Trump could be trusted to bring about the radical change our country needed.

Afterward, I showed her my changes to the script. I had crossed out parts I didn't think were strong and added the phrase: *Let's make history and elect him president.*

"Hmm…" Maddy said while she read it. She looked up and smiled. "I like that! We'll use it."

"Really?" I was surprised she made the decision so quickly. "You don't have to take it to some committee or something?"

She chuckled. "No. I make those decisions and I really like what you've done," she said. "Thank you so much for taking the time."

A sense of optimism came over me. Could it be that maybe, just maybe, being part of this campaign would feel completely different from my other forays into political activism for third-party candidates? I had always known that, despite my efforts, my candidate would always lose. The continual losses had worn on me. But this time might be different. Maybe I could back someone who might actually win!

But then I paused. I didn't like the idea of joining the Republican Party. I didn't trust the GOP any more than I did the Democrats. On the other hand, Trump seemed like someone who was not only willing to obliterate the established political order but actually seemed able to do so.

I can't recall the exact moment, but at some point that afternoon I made a life-altering decision: I joined the group. I became one of them—because they were supporting an outsider. I decided I was going to work to elect Trump president.

From that day forward, I began making phone calls across the country with the script I helped create. I recruited people to vote for Trump and showed them where to get registered. People would tell me, "Rich, you're a valuable member of the team." It was a good feeling, one I'd never experienced before. For the first time in my life I was part of something bigger than me. It was out of character but irresistible. I told myself, "Trump is your candidate. These are your people. This is where you belong."

CHAPTER 3
Freefalling into MAGA

Trump addressed all three of my gripes.

First, what he said rang true to me. I related to someone who seemed comfortable in his own skin—a son of a bitch who didn't care what anyone thought of him. Trump inspired me. I felt like he spoke my language. Supporting him would definitely shake things up and that's exactly what I wanted. Wrongs would be righted. This would finally be my chance to make a difference in people's lives and deliver political power into the hands of everyday Americans. *Check!*

Second was Trump's success as a businessman. He was so wealthy that he didn't need to rely on donations from large corporations or special interests. His vows to "drain the swamp" and "destroy the Deep State" hit the mark. *Check!*

Third, his campaign dispelled my lifelong sense of alienation. I looked around the room and thought, "These people see things the same way I do!" I hadn't known such a group existed. My intense hatred for the two major parties left me eager to embrace the MAGA mindset. I ate up everything MAGA fed me, without questioning any of it. The empathy I had developed for the homeless and underprivileged motivated me to support Trump. He would speak for all of us who had been left behind by traditional politics. *Check!*

———◆———

Who could I trust to tell me the truth? Donald J. Trump!

He routinely denounced mainstream media as "fake news," so I dutifully cut out all sources of information that were not full-on Trump supporters. I rabidly increased my intake of Fox News and Rush Limbaugh. My primary source of information was a website I'd rarely perused before Trump: Breitbart. It was filled with articles and commentary that fed my growing panic about the creeping socialism and communism that would take over the country if Democrats won the election.

I fully embraced MAGA's "us vs. them" worldview. *They* were out to get me and my family. *They* wanted to take control of the country and never leave office. *They* were coming for our guns (even though I didn't have one). I obsessively pored over the Breitbart comments section, which hammered away at the evils of my enemies.

Who were *they*? Democrats. Socialists. Communists. Political elites. They had already weaponized the federal government by building a bureaucracy of so-called experts who freely imposed their will on the American people. This was "the Deep State," in which dark forces concocted schemes to deprive us of our freedoms.

As Trump gained strength in the campaign, a number of traditional Republicans left the party, calling themselves Never Trumpers. The emergence of this group only reinforced my belief that the system had always been corrupt. These Republicans were deserting their conservative values and joining the Democrats in all their nefarious schemes.

> *I fully embraced MAGA's "us vs. them" worldview. They were out to get me and my family. They wanted to take control of the country and never leave office.*

Trump argued for a Muslim ban and for building a wall that he claimed Mexico would pay for. MAGA pundits trumpeted the Great Replacement Theory, a supposed plot by Democrats to reduce the influence and power of white Americans through mass immigration. From every corner of the MAGA echo chamber came the terrifying message that millions of illegal immigrants were invading and that among them were terrorists, rapists, drug dealers, and murderers. I believed all of it.

Trump's minions thundered that "Democrats are coming for your guns!" I became convinced that the Democrats were intent on taking our Second Amendment rights away— a message drummed into me at every turn. Terrified that I wouldn't be able to protect my family from *them*, I bought my first handgun, and then an AR-15-style automatic rifle.

Religious themes bolstered MAGA's claims that America was a Christian nation, built by and for Christians, based on Biblical laws and morality. Example after example was given to support the idea that American society was in moral decline, aided by foreign religions and immigrant cultures. Pastors and prophets surrounded Trump with prayer and promises of God's blessing. Even though I was raised Catholic and wasn't an active participant, the concerns expressed by evangelical Protestants increased my fears.

I came to agree with the apocalyptic warnings that the threat was existential. Democrats wouldn't be satisfied with winning the election—they planned to keep power indefinitely by coming for our children. Planned Parenthood killed babies for profit, and women couldn't be trusted to make moral decisions. *Roe v. Wade* had to be overturned.

The LGBTQ+ community wanted to turn our children transgender by infesting our schools with their obscene books. Trans people, specifically trans women, wanted to invade women's public bathrooms and unfairly compete in sports. Feminism had undermined societal stability by persuading women to pursue careers over motherhood, creating an epidemic of divorce and single-parent families.

> *Pastors and prophets surrounded Trump with prayer and promises of God's blessing. Even though I was raised Catholic and wasn't an active participant, the concerns expressed by evangelical Protestants increased my fears.*

Democratic indoctrination threatened the foundations of our public education system. Under the guise of ethnic studies, America's enemies spread subversive ideas like Critical Race Theory—never mind that I had never researched it or understood what it taught. They bombarded us with false theories of "white fragility," and blamed people living in the 21st century for slavery.

How could we defeat this massive onslaught of immoral, power-hungry people? Donald J. Trump. He would make it right. Stand up for us. Drain the swamp. Expose and destroy the Deep State.

The more I obsessed over these messages of anger, fear, and loyalty, the more laser-focused I became. I was convinced that a Clinton victory would permanently give the Democrats national political power. Having been alienated from our two major parties for years, this fear was quite palpable for me. A Clinton win would forever quash any chance of my being heard by the government. I would be invisible forever.

If I had no impact, I would lose control of my ability to provide for my family and keep them safe. I wasn't just your average MAGA American. I became an obsessed political activist, utterly devoted to Donald Trump.

I even did something I never expected I would do—change my voter registration from Independent to Republican. This might seem like a small thing, but it was perhaps the most telling of all the changes I made. My identity as an American man was rooted in seeing myself as independent of the bipartisan sham. To formally join the Republican

Party was to admit I had become part of something I had hated my entire adult life.

But if that was what Trump needed from me, I would do it. Time was running out before the November election. I had to make up for lost time. My loyalty to Trump pushed me down a path I had been determined to never take.

———◆———

I had built up a huge reservoir of resentment against the two-party system over the years, and now I channeled all those intense feelings into hatred of Democrats and those Republicans who had betrayed the MAGA cause. My new identity and sense of belonging caused me to cut off contact with those outside the MAGA community. People I'd known for years, including my mentor Carl, were shunted aside. I simply didn't trust their opinions anymore.

My embrace of MAGA rested on a foundation of perceived danger, and my fear of outsiders intensified every time I met with the volunteers for Trump's campaign. Collectively we discredited anyone who disagreed with those of us in the know. We shared stories of the latest ways our country was under assault by socialists, communists, and political elites who only cared about themselves. Our enemies list steadily grew.

> *I had built up a huge reservoir of resentment against the two-party system over the years, and now I channeled all those intense feelings into hatred of Democrats and those Republicans who had betrayed the MAGA cause.*

It's important to acknowledge that good and decent people were and still are part of the MAGA movement. It's like a large and loyal family—a tribe, a clan. Friendships blossomed. Even outside of campaign activities, we hung out and shared meals together. We trusted each other. And we *were* trustworthy—as long as someone was part of our close-knit group. We clung to each other largely out of fear.

My sense of righteous anger at our political adversaries grew exponentially. They were beneath human dignity, people who deserved to be punished in the most severe ways. My MAGA journey may have just been in its beginning stages, but it progressed with lightning speed, fueled by fear that quickly turned into hate that controlled me for years.

It seemed the press was parroting the lies and tactics of the Democratic Party and anti-Trump Republicans. I began to see the national media as what Trump said it was: a de facto publicist for the Democrats and Hillary Clinton. I loathed her more than anyone.

Nothing changed for me when Trump served up a litany of offensive comments: the "blood coming out of her wherever" comment about Megyn Kelly; hinting at setting up a registry of Muslims; belittling the Gold Star parents of a soldier who died while serving in Iraq; and, perhaps most infamously, the Access Hollywood tape.

I saw his rhetoric as proof of his brashness and willingness to break the rules in order to drain the swamp. This was exactly what we needed—someone strong enough to do the job. I didn't want some "politically correct" weakling.

Rather than being offended, we laughed at his comments. Some didn't take them seriously and excused Trump with, "Well, boys will be boys." Others just shrugged, offering no criticism. I dutifully accepted and defended every word. After all, we were in a war to save our democracy from pernicious forces. The alternative to Trump was not just a worse candidate, but an enemy who needed to be destroyed.

> *My sense of righteous anger at our political adversaries grew exponentially. They were beneath human dignity, people who deserved to be punished in the most severe ways.*

There was no room for ideas like bipartisan cooperation or political negotiations or compromise. I was a zealous acolyte, singularly intent on victory. Let me say this again so there can be no question of my goal: *My intention was to destroy the enemy. I was willing to use my platform and growing influence to do just that.*

CHAPTER 4
A Full-Blown MAGA Star

During one of my weekly segments on American Workers Radio, I offered a daring prediction: "I have my ear to the ground, and I can tell you without a shadow of a doubt that Donald Trump will be our next president!"

Most people loudly rejected my forecast. *There's no way that Trump can beat Clinton!*

I countered, "I talk to everyone, and I do mean everyone whom I meet during my day. The mail carrier, at the doctor's office, with business associates, at the checkout line, and there are more Trump supporters than you think. Many feel shamed by the left, and they don't want to be ridiculed. But they lean over and whisper to me, 'I'm voting for Trump.' You wait and see. He'll win!"

My view was not the norm, even among those in the campaign. Most were discouraged by the pushback against Trump in the media and among their friends and family members. Angry arguments left relationships damaged. But as others despaired, I had a good feeling in my gut.

Despite my confidence, and even though I wasn't the most religious Catholic, the night before the election I drove to a nearby church, sat in the dark parking lot and said a prayer for victory: "Dear God, let us be victorious tomorrow."

———◆———

Election night arrived! I sat on the couch with my wife and watched the returns. Living on the East Coast, we always have to stay up later for the polls to close in other areas of the country.

The evening started off as expected. Blue states went to Clinton and red states went to Trump. My wife expressed concern about my being disappointed, but I held firmly to my prediction. Nevertheless, I was expecting a long, long night of back and forth.

And then, key states like Pennsylvania and Michigan went for Trump. Even though I had insisted publicly that he would win, it was thrilling. And then the map became redder and redder. My phone lit up with texts. People started calling me. Emails flooded in.

"You got it right!"

"How did you know?"

"I shouldn't have doubted you!"

My wife went to bed while I fielded phone calls and answered texts from people across the country who had heard my prediction. Trump was going to win and…I'd been right! I was exhilarated!

Past midnight and into the early morning, the calls, texts, and emails poured in. My wife got up around 3 a.m. to see what was going on. She was delighted, not so much about Trump winning, but because she supported me.

I was on the phone until close to 5 a.m. I got a couple of hours sleep and then got up early for my radio appearance. It was Wednesday, after all. I tried to be humble, but I'll admit I reveled in the astonished accolades heaped upon me that day.

———◆———

Trump won!

We won! But more than that…*I won!*

It was like I had put on a new pair of glasses and politics looked different to me now. After Trump took office in 2017, my enthusiasm grew. Even though he was now president, I saw my role in MAGA expanding, not decreasing. There was no time to rest on our laurels. Yes, the Democrats had lost *this* election, but what about the midterms and the presidential election after that? I was determined to do all I could to increase MAGA's influence and defeat all political foes.

I began writing opinion pieces. I researched media platforms and submitted my work, and got published in *The Federalist, American Thinker, American Greatness, WorldNetDaily, RealClearPolitics, The Daily Caller*, and even *Fox News*.

Here's a sampling of my headlines:
- "Democrat Cities: Fourth-World Scourges"
- "#MeToo: Then and Now, an Epic Farce"

- "Democrats' Trump Impeachment Push Is a Bonanza for Republicans"
- "Pete Buttigieg: Dumbest Ever Smart Person?"
- "Bernard Sanders: Stretch Limousine Liberal"
- "Some Congressional Expulsions Are in Order"
- "Welcome to the Democrat Freak Show"
- "Will Today's Voters Be Offended by Trump's 'Nationalism'?"
- "Vicious Democrat Lie: The GOP Stole Obama's Supreme Court Seat"
- "Gun Lies, Myths, Half-Truths, and Conspiracy Theories"
- "Beware the Blue Wave"
- "Is James Comey Insane?"

Trump's enemies were my enemies. I took offense at any criticism thrown his way. And whenever he said or did something controversial that got a rise out of his opponents, I was ready with an explanation and, if there wasn't one, an excuse. I knew deep down his victory was for the greater good.

———◆———

Warning! This is the Rich Logis show. The content you are about to hear has been deemed dangerous and inappropriate to Democrats and Tessio Republicans. Listener discretion is advised. And now your host and equal opportunity offender, Rich Logis!

I also became a MAGA podcaster. A "Tessio Republican" was a Never Trumper; the term referred to Sal Tessio, the character in *The Godfather* who betrays Michael Corleone after he becomes Don. Here's how I opened each episode:

"This is Rich Logis, and here you get four-dimensional commentary and analysis. Other shows offer only three dimensions, the ones you can already see. But there's a fourth dimension that we bring to you. There's always that fourth dimension. What is that? There is always more going on in the background. We bring what's hidden to the forefront.

"I've done the deep dive in my research that you don't have time to do, and what other shows don't take the trouble to do. We care about you, want you to be informed and thank you for being so loyal. You'll only find out what's really happening by tuning into this show."

I put my spin on every theme that MAGA had drilled into my head. As an aspiring pundit, I desperately wanted the president's attention. My unspoken dream, of course, was to become influential enough to get noticed. To gain Trump's favor, I modeled my persona after his—hostile, mocking, and arrogant. I also learned from him to never apologize, regardless of the size of a mistake or the damage caused by anyone in the MAGA world. And I never did apologize for anything during that time in my life.

And why would I? The more outrageous the claim and the more demeaning I could be of our opponents, the better I felt about myself. To be honest with you, underneath the bluster, I was terrified. I'd been convinced that the demographics were racing toward a multiracial and cultural tsunami that would leave me, as a white man, unable to protect my family from the destruction that would be inflicted on us by the Democrats.

I hammered the message that we would soon be outnumbered and lose the America we believed in to the socialist, anti-democratic agenda. I was decidedly an America First nationalist who drew a direct line from the Constitution and my rights to Donald Trump, who understood our needs and would set the country in the right direction. And I do mean right—as far right as I could make happen.

Any semblance of third-party independence had been sacrificed on the altar of Trump's power. Motivated by the need to obliterate any influence exerted by MAGA's enemies, of which there were many, my team and I produced over 150 episodes. Achieving this massive body of work took hundreds of hours of my time and cost me a fortune—thousands upon thousands of dollars. But it was worth it to me. MAGA was my second family, and I used funds that would have otherwise gone to my first family. As far as I was concerned, there was no sacrifice too great or investment too large when it came to my utter devotion to Donald Trump.

I spent hours researching, late into the night. The podcasts might have sounded like I was talking off the cuff, but I knew exactly what I was going to say—the details, the talking points I wanted to hit. I labored to ensure every word had the right spin, a spin I believed was uniquely mine.

> As far as I was concerned, there was no sacrifice too great or investment too large when it came to my utter devotion to Donald Trump.

I now understand that my sense of reality was distorted, but no one could have convinced me of that at the time. I sincerely believed that Trump, and only Trump, could protect us from the enemy from within. We were surrounded by traitors who intended us harm.

During the episode about the Second Amendment, I said: "What I've discovered with the Second Amendment is the Democrats have a blood thirst for infringing upon people's freedoms. They want us to live in fear of the government.

"But the truth is, the government fears the people. So they want to take away all of our guns. Then when the feds come for us, we'll have no way to defend ourselves. The government under the Democrats wants more power. We know that the state is already failing and they just want more. They don't want an abundance of liberty, but liberty is what we are ultimately about here at the Rich Logis show."

Although abortion wasn't one of my major issues, I nicknamed Bernie Sanders Mao Zed, a none-too-subtle reference to Chinese dictator Mao Zedong. I was associating Sanders with China's pernicious One-Child Policy, which included forced abortion. I had actually mangled the joke, because Beijing didn't unveil the policy until three years after Mao died. But hewing strictly to the facts mattered less than scoring political points. I felt no compunction about comparing Democrats and Never Trump Republicans to mass murderers.

I claimed that bipartisanship was the gateway drug to tyranny—that American politics was essentially kill or be killed. On an episode about the battle for conservative control of the Supreme Court, I said, "We're beating Democrat judicial activism. But here's the real question for all of us. How greedy are we now? Are we greedy enough to run up the score?

"You know, in the Super Bowl I've seen teams that are there for the first time, and they're just happy to be there. And they might do all right at the beginning, but they typically lose. Are we really committed to running up the score against the Democrats and their judges? And I'm not just talking about the Supreme Court, but about the federal judiciary as well. We need to be as greedy as possible."

I went on: "If you're a Republican who sides against us, you're a Democrat. Everyone has to take a side. If you're not siding with America First and nationalism, then you're not being a true American."

My basic message was consistent—the Democrats wanted to "update" the Constitution rather than preserve its original intent. And if that happened, we would lose everything.

The bottom line was this: *Democrats are out to take your children, your money, and your freedoms. No one outside of MAGA can be trusted. Only Donald Trump can save us.*

PART 2

Leaving MAGA

From True Believer to the Trauma of Betrayal

———◆———

2016-2022

CHAPTER 5

The First Crack of Betrayal

Election of 2020

Election day, November 3, 2020, was a mere five days after the glorious banquet where I'd enjoyed rubbing shoulders with the MAGA elite at Mar-a-Lago. I met a couple friends for dinner. We chose a place that had a television so we could watch the returns.

The polls were about to close in Florida as we settled into our chairs, abuzz with the expectation of another victory. I tried to hold onto the optimism I felt at Mar-a-Lago, but as we ordered our drinks and entrées, I could no longer ignore the gnawing doubt inside. I kept my misgivings to myself as the evening began, but soon the gloom of a possible loss fell over us.

Around 10 p.m., we left the restaurant and went to a friend's house. We poured drinks, still clinging desperately to the hope that we would toast Trump's reelection. We remained steadfast even as various outlets predicted a Biden win, but our confident bravado abruptly turned into angry disbelief when, at 11:20 p.m., Fox News projected that Arizona—a state Trump won in 2016—had flipped to the Democratic nominee. There was still about twenty-five percent of the vote left to count.

"What is Fox doing?" one of my friends yelled at the TV. Had our own cherished network betrayed MAGA? No, we knew what this meant. Our drinks would be for drowning our sorrow. There would be no toast to victory.

The clock passed midnight and Biden came out to tell his supporters to have patience because he believed they would eventually win. More bad news continued into the early hours of the morning. At around 2:30 a.m., the president addressed his supporters at the White House. Trump declared himself the winner. "We'll be going to the U.S. Supreme Court," he said. "We want all voting to stop. We don't want them to find any ballots at four o'clock in the morning and add them to the list."

Trump insisted that his voters—indeed the whole country—were the victims of an unprecedented fraud, perpetrated by Biden and the Democrats. His voice filled the room. "We were getting ready to win this election. Frankly, we *did* win this election."

I dropped my head into my hands. He wasn't going to accept the results. I thought this was a huge mistake. It was painful watching him bluster. I'd had enough. I bid goodbye to my crestfallen friends and headed for home.

———◆———

About fifteen minutes later, I quietly unlocked the door to my house and tried to enter without waking my wife and daughters. The adrenaline that had propelled me through Election Day was gone, replaced by a deep fatigue.

I carefully pulled out the handgun I had tucked into the back of my trousers. I often carried a concealed weapon, which was legal in Florida. I had taken it with me out of concern that if Trump won, some local Democrats might act up and I'd need to protect myself.

> Trump insisted that his voters—indeed the whole country—were the victims of an unprecedented fraud, perpetrated by Biden and the Democrats. His voice filled the room. "We were getting ready to win this election. Frankly, we did win this election."

Because I had two young children, I was always very careful with my weapons. With the television droning in the background, I opened the gun cabinet, put the handgun back in its case next to my AR-15-style rifle, and locked it.

Standing in the entryway, I debated whether to turn on the TV or just go to bed. My curiosity got the best of me, so I flipped on the election coverage. Flopping down in front of the TV, my stomach turned at the sight of Trump's falling numbers. I was devastated. What would happen now, with the Democrats back in power? Would they *ever* leave the White House again? Would they turn America into a communist state as Trump had predicted?

Although the election results terrified me, I remained a pragmatist. I immediately set aside my despair, ignored my exhaustion, and started strategizing. How could we turn this defeat into victory in 2024? We had to limit these treacherous villains to one term.

The country needed to learn that it had made a mistake. Trump had made strides while in office, but the swamp of corruption endured. The federal bureaucracy, an uncontrollable beast that ate our tax dollars, still inflicted its "woke" agenda on Americans. I worked feverishly to come up with ways I could help protect the MAGA brand and lay the groundwork for a Trump comeback.

Four years earlier on election night, I had basked in the euphoria of winning, fielding calls and texts from my MAGA compatriots who congratulated me on my prediction of victory. When the Associated Press confirmed Fox's prediction that Biden would win Arizona, I turned off the TV. I couldn't take anymore. Barely awake and deeply discouraged, I shuffled off to bed.

◆

With no more evidence than Trump's declaration, MAGA loudly proclaimed the election had been stolen. Over the next several weeks, I held onto a sliver of hope as the Trump campaign's legal team and its allies fired off dozens of lawsuits aimed at the key swing states he had lost. If they uncovered evidence of massive and systemic voter fraud, I would be the first to stand up and support Trump without hesitation. But I resisted the allure of believing in a miracle.

On December 11, the Supreme Court extinguished Trump's last legal hope when it threw out Texas' lawsuit challenging the results in Georgia, Michigan, Wisconsin and Pennsylvania. Even though I was unsurprised, the full weight of the loss hit me hard. I thought of the enormous sacrifices I'd made over the past four years—the endless hours spent producing my podcast, writing articles, speaking at events. I'd done all I could to keep MAGA in power.

A dark despair settled over me that had nothing to do with losing the election. It was about Trump refusing to acknowledge he had lost. Sometimes you lose elections. God knows I'd spent plenty of election nights with my third-party candidates who had gone down to defeat. We had reached a critical moment for MAGA, and the world was watching us. We needed Trump to lead—*I* needed Trump to lead—with dignity and humility, not to act like a sore loser, throwing tantrums like a child who didn't get his way.

Yet why would I expect anything else? Trump never conceded defeat. He never apologized. If something went wrong, he always blamed someone else. Of course Trump would refuse to accept the truth and instead promote a bald-faced lie. I'd never admitted to anyone, let alone to myself, that Trump continually lied. But this time I faced reality. *I knew that he knew he had lost—and chose to lie about it.*

> **"** *We needed Trump to lead— I needed Trump to lead—with dignity and humility, not to act like a sore loser, throwing tantrums like a child who didn't get his way.*

Everyone in MAGA was supposed to follow along, support him, and perpetuate his lie. Many in the movement believed Trump's claims of voter fraud, or at the very least deluded themselves into believing them. Those of us who didn't felt pressured to support him anyway. What did the truth matter when we had a larger goal of saving America?

Even though I didn't echo Trump's claim to a stolen election, I wasn't about to leave over this awful turn of events. I still believed he was America's only hope. I convinced myself Trump would realize how his election lies were an affront to democracy itself. He'd certainly deflected his share of arrows during his political career. If he changed course now, the election lie would fade from the public's memory and we could pivot to prepare for the 2024 election.

———◆———

I didn't feel particularly festive welcoming in 2021. And the bad news kept coming.

On January 3, *The Washington Post* published a recording of an hour-long phone call held the day before in which Trump pressured Georgia Secretary of State Brad Raffensperger to "find" enough votes to flip the state to the president. I heard the desperation in Trump's voice, and imagined how hard it must have been for Raffensperger to insist the results were valid. Not only had Trump lied about losing the election, now he was trying to overturn the outcome. Another crack of betrayal spread among the bricks that held me captive.

By the time Trump rallied his supporters in Washington, DC on January 6, I had no desire to attend. I just wanted the election madness to be over. Instead, Trump called on Vice President Mike Pence to refuse to certify the election and sent the crowd to the Capitol. The hangman's noose was on full display. As the rioters breached the building, I was apoplectic—not because the police were violently over-whelmed, and not because people were getting hurt (I looked away as those scenes unfolded). I was outraged because the invaders were ruining Trump's chances in 2024. To make matters worse, the president didn't denounce them or call out the National Guard to stop them. His behavior infuriated me. *Why was he undermining the brand that I'd worked so hard to build?*

I doubled down on my devotion to Trump. My weekly stints on *American Workers Radio* turned into angry rants against the press and Democrats for their obsession with January 6. I loudly pushed the narrative that the president's critics were blowing this small riot way out of proportion. I ridiculed those who said January 6 was as historically significant as Pearl Harbor and Sept. 11.

I joked that the federal government prosecuted some of the rioters as if they were criminal masterminds. I insisted they were just a small group acting on their own, and that Trump was not responsible.

But deep down, I was in turmoil. To protect myself from the truth, I stopped watching the January 6 coverage.

One morning, I woke up and felt an almost imperceptible stab of pain in my gut. I tried to ignore it, but I couldn't. I knew what had happened. The bond I had forged with Trump, the connection I thought was unbreakable, had fractured ever so slightly.

But that couldn't be true! I lived inside the safety of MAGA—a fortress hewn out of one single flawless chunk of marble with a gold-plated statue of Donald Trump atop the battlements. It was indestructible.

Yet light shone through that tiny crack and I saw that MAGA was not an impenetrable fortress. It was a prison I had built, brick by brick, lie after lie, held together by my devoted trust and desperate fervor.

If I'd had the power, I would have forgotten this stark flash of recognition.

The bond I had forged with Trump, the connection I thought was unbreakable, had fractured ever so slightly.

I didn't want anything to change. Never had I felt so alive or empowered as during my time in the MAGA community. I wanted to excuse Trump's lies as "exaggerations," or blame them on the mainstream media's "fake news."

But I couldn't. Not this time. Trump hadn't simply lied; I was used to that. No, this lie put the foundation of democracy at risk. This lie was a betrayal of the country I loved. This lie was personal; Trump had betrayed me.

CHAPTER 6
My Year of Heaven and Hell

As Joe Biden was sworn into office on January 20, 2021, fear and loathing pulsated through me. What would happen to MAGA now with Trump causing chaos over the election and the Democrats taking back the White House?

One might think that the deep betrayal I felt would have turned me against Trump, but the opposite actually happened. The reality of having Democrats in power triggered such a deep anxiety that I threw myself into attacking the left with renewed venom.

Hearing the mantra *they're coming for your guns* in the back of my mind, I wrote two freelance articles in March 2021 for *American Greatness*, both of which focused on gun violence. On March 12, I wrote a piece that blamed Democrats for the 2018 massacre at Marjory Stoneman Douglas High School in Parkland, Florida.

"Democrats effectively have seized upon the survivors' unfathomable grief for their own nefarious political gain," I asserted. "[E]specially loathsome and sinister has been the thrusting of traumatized children into the roles of activists, force-feeding them the usual Democratic and media propaganda from the anti-gun cult."

Ten days later, I published an essay challenging the narrative that the man who killed eight people at two spas and a massage parlor in Atlanta was motivated by anti-Asian hate. I based my conclusion on a spurious statistical analysis, then launched into my main argument: Democrats falsely create hate crime narratives "to keep the eyes of aggrieved members of their respective minority groups on the prize: payback against whites."

I fanned the flames of fear about the danger I predicted would soon come down on the MAGA community at the hands of those I had despised for years.

———◆———

As far as my MAGA community was concerned, I supported Trump as staunchly as ever—maybe even more. They didn't seem to notice that I never chimed in when declaring that the 2020 election had been stolen. During the day, I played the role of true believer. I went to lunch with close MAGA friends and declared, "The liberals from New York are coming!" I echoed whatever Trump said. The last thing I wanted to do was draw attention to the fissures opening up between us. I did all I could to hide the pain of betrayal I felt. But at night, holed up with my doubts, I warred with myself.

When I first boarded the Trump Train, I bought my ticket to a place where I thought America would be great again. No more Deep State or corrupt elites ruling with impunity while sucking the life out of the middle class. People in MAGA shared a vision of economic growth and a common identity: We were the *real* Americans. We flew the flag with patriotic pride and wore our red hats and T-shirts so everyone would know we were unabashedly aligned with Donald J. Trump. We were *the people* and MAGA was the people's movement.

But now, I saw myself as a hapless traveler who bought a ticket in 2016 for a bright and beautiful destination, only to discover in 2021 that the train had instead taken me to a dark and foreboding outpost. I'd believed that Trump would save democracy from *them*. He would drain the swamp, not jump into the deep end *with* them. He sent an armed group of nationalists to stop the peaceful transfer of power. How could I claim he was protecting democracy when he was willing to destroy it to retain power?

> *But now, I saw myself as a hapless traveler who bought a ticket in 2016 for a bright and beautiful destination, only to discover in 2021 that the train had instead taken me to a dark and foreboding outpost.*

During months of sleepless nights, memories flooded in: The euphoria of election night 2016. The adrenaline rush of seeing my articles published on right-wing websites. How I flippantly disregarded the attack on the Capitol.

Questions haunted me with the relentlessness of Scrooge's ghosts. *Have I been deceived this entire time? Has this whole thing been a con to get power he never intended to relinquish? If so, what will I do? Where can I go? Who would I support?*

I felt shame about the choices I'd made. Tossing and turning in bed, I wondered how I could have given Trump my undying loyalty. *When did I morph from a man of principle who defended democracy into someone who would spin the truth to protect a politician?* It felt like a slow and tedious bloodletting by a million paper cuts.

As the questions swirled in my mind, I anxiously worried that my friends would notice my personal and political turmoil. At the same time, it distressed me that they were promoting Trump's lies. Still, I knew if I voiced my concerns, they would reject me. I would be tossed out and lose everything I'd built for the past several years. With Trump, there is no room for forgiveness, no do-overs, no options for making amends.

If I walked away, I'd be on my own, an object of ridicule. I would be branded a traitor. As I thought about leaving MAGA, I imagined standing on an empty train platform in the middle of nowhere all by myself. I had no idea where I was, or which direction to go. If another train showed up, I wouldn't want to get on board. After all, I despised the Democrats and the rest of *them*. My anxiety intensified.

> *If I walked away, I'd be on my own, an object of ridicule. I would be branded a traitor.*

My MAGA world was crumbling into dust, but I could not imagine a future without it. I didn't want to give up my friends, my community. I saw the truth, but I tried to ignore it, silence it, deny it. I kept my doubts to myself.

I formed Save Our Sunshine State, a super political action committee. Its goal was to motivate as many Floridians as possible to register to vote as Republicans. I wrote a weekly newsletter, explaining how important it was to counter the COVID-inspired influx of people from California, New York, and other blue states. Failure meant the state would become "unaffordable, unsafe, and unfree."

I sent letters to Florida and national GOP leaders urging them to pay attention to my super PAC, without success. We did get some press: the *Sun Sentinel* and a local CBS TV affiliate did stories about us.

Channeling my energy into Save Our Sunshine State helped me deal with the severe disappointment of losing the White House. It also served as a distraction from the nagging doubts about MAGA that surfaced after the election and January 6.

After COVID first broke out in 2020, I followed Trump's lead about the virus and didn't take it seriously. I often held my sleeping baby girl in one arm while I wrote an opinion piece with my free hand on my phone. I mocked senior citizens in particular, joking that grandma and grandpa were living in COVID fallout shelters. I thought forcing people to wear masks to protect them and others was silly and unnecessary. I wore masks only when I patronized businesses that mandated them.

At the same time, I understood the need to protect the public, particularly with a vaccine. In the months after the pandemic erupted, my governor, Ron DeSantis, impressed me with his leadership. He was a staunch proponent of vaccination. In a widely circulated photograph from December 2020, DeSantis pushes a wheelchair-bound elderly woman to get vaccinated.

I got my first COVID vaccine in April 2021, followed by the second dose when it became available. I felt immense pride observing the crowded waiting area; I considered Operation Warp Speed Trump's landmark achievement. But given the widespread anti-vax beliefs within MAGA, I only told a few people I'd gotten the shots.

I excused the president's altercations with Dr. Anthony Fauci, and his touting untried treatments such as bleach and hydrochloroquine. I never bought into the wackier conspiracy theories around COVID; I knew it wasn't a bioweapon manufactured by sinister forces to prevent Trump's reelection.

> *After COVID first broke out in 2020, I followed Trump's lead about the virus and didn't take it seriously. I often held my sleeping baby girl in one arm while I wrote an opinion piece with my free hand on my phone.*

In August 2021, COVID deaths from the Delta variant surged in Florida and other states. Florida had one of the highest infection rates in the nation. As the father of two young girls, I was especially unnerved by the overcrowding at children's hospitals. Kids were dying.

A few weeks later, DeSantis held a news conference in the small town of Newberry to voice his opposition to vaccine mandates. Two of the speakers claimed the COVID vaccine changed a person's RNA, and was more likely to kill or injure an individual than the disease itself. DeSantis stood quietly, saying nothing to counter the vaccine voodoo polemics.

When asked the next day about the outrageous remarks, DeSantis said he didn't remember what the speakers had said. Not only had he allowed anti-vaxxers to regurgitate debunked conspiracy theories, but by claiming not to remember their remarks, he insulted my intelligence.

The images were emblazoned on my mind: Desperate parents of COVID-stricken children huddled in intensive care units. Parents going to morgues to collect their kids' bodies. *What if one of my girls gets infected? What is DeSantis doing to protect my daughters?*

I pried out the brick called FLORIDA'S COVID RESPONSE from the MAGA wall and threw it to the ground. More light streamed in. While the wall still held, it was beginning to wobble quite a bit.

CHAPTER 7

The MAGA Wall Falls

I made a decision. A big one, by MAGA standards. I resolved to change my information diet, a violation of one of MAGA's cardinal rules.

I ventured outside my insular circle of "acceptable" outlets and explored what we had deemed "fake news," or what I had dubbed the DMIC—the Democrat Media Industrial Complex: *The New York Times*, *The Washington Post*, *The Atlantic*, and *The Guardian* of London. I even examined the writings of socialists and communists.

I quickly discovered that some of DeSantis' staffers had trafficked in outlandish anti-vax conspiracy theories involving the "biomedical security state," with (of course) "the Jews" in charge. DeSantis had clearly pivoted to irresponsible extremism on COVID as a way to position himself for a presidential run in 2024. I had thought he was a man of principles, but he had shown himself to be the opposite.

My disgust with DeSantis led me to turn over a stone I had deliberately left unturned for eight months: January 6. At first I hesitated; perhaps subconsciously, I knew what I would find.

The crowd besieging the Capitol included members of the Proud Boys, the Oath Keepers, and the Three Percenters. I had always dismissed them as fringe hobbyists—hangers-on who treated politics as an excuse to socialize. After Trump told the Proud Boys during a debate to "stand back and stand by," I rolled my eyes at the resulting uproar; yet again, the mainstream media were making a big deal out of nothing. Trump-inspired violent extremists? Yawn. But as I read the accounts of what happened on January 6, I realized these groups were far from irrelevant.

Trump hadn't renounced them because they were his *allies*. They had the blessing of the most powerful person in the world. That meant they had been my allies, as well. What had I done? How could I have missed this?

The protestors and police who died during and after the attack on the Capitol would still be alive if not for Trump. And I was complicit. I felt rage, confusion, shock, and, most acutely, shame. I deserved to be inextricably linked to the militias I had once yawned at.

My discoveries underscored why preventing people from consuming—or believing—independent journalism is central to MAGA's political approach. What happens and what it means are carefully curated in the MAGA media echo chamber. Straying from the approved sources of information threatens the movement's entire edifice.

Because I had exclusively consumed MAGA-approved media for years, I had no idea how much important information had been omitted from my news feed. I suddenly understood why those outside of MAGA were confounded by insiders' responses to their arguments. It wasn't that I had a different interpretation of events—I wasn't even aware that certain things had happened. This realization shook me to the core.

Although I had diligently invested many hours researching MAGA sources for my writing and podcasts, I never stood a chance of getting things right because I had cut myself off from any information outside the bubble. I had shaped my perspective on the world through self-censorship.

My situation struck me as strangely familiar, and I realized it mirrored my childhood experience. By ignoring every major conflict and crisis at home and abroad, my parents had normalized the idea of living in isolation from certain information. No wonder the MAGA silo felt so comfortable, so much like home.

For years, I had parroted MAGA talking points as if I were quoting sacred Scriptures. Now the spreading cracks in the wall enabled me to pull out one brick at a time, examine it, and decide if I'd keep it or not. Over the next year, that's exactly what I did. It was an excruciating process—swinging back and forth between my conscience and my community.

> *For years, I had parroted MAGA talking points as if I were quoting sacred Scriptures.*

I read articles and essays from all sides of the issues, opening my mind to viewpoints I'd discounted in the past. I reexamined my beliefs about abortion, the LGBTQ+ community, education, and immigrants. I realized left-wing extremists were not planning to turn America into a communist gulag.

I reflected on the many traumas our country has endured since the turn of the century, including 9/11, the invasions of Afghanistan and Iraq, the Great Recession, and the pandemic. As I thought back on all these painful episodes, I added Trump to the list. He had seduced about a third of the country, including me. He had turned America away from democracy. I had been duped by a bait-and-switch and had helped foster division for Trump's political benefit.

Who had I become? I was no longer the person I'd been in college, focused on dialogue and community service. All of that had vanished. Somewhere along the way, I shifted from my commitment to democracy to protecting MAGA. *Where was my moral center?*

> *He had seduced about a third of the country, including me. He had turned America away from democracy.*

It was now May 2022. Thinking about college brought to mind my old mentor, Dr. Carl Procario-Foley. I'd kept in touch with him over the years, although I never mentioned my passion for Trump. I knew he was a Democrat, so I didn't want to risk losing our friendship. And since Carl didn't follow MAGA influencers in Florida, he had no way to know about my pivot to political extremism.

Despite our vastly different perspectives, I felt I could trust him to help me sort through my existential questions. I emailed him, detailing my life in MAGA. I also attached a letter I had written to myself.

In it, I endeavored to define a leader: "One who never asks others to do what he/she doesn't do. One who is always honest, even at the risk of losing relationships and money. One who retains his beliefs, even when holding on to those beliefs is not expedient or beneficial."

A leader should allow himself to be challenged, I wrote. "If you change your mind on an issue, great. If not, also great. No one forms his opinions and beliefs wholly without influence…When many around us are screaming in neck vein-popping fashion, those who take a serene, even-tempered approach will stand out."

I professed a desire to become "a born-again human being. In a political context, we can realize this by acknowledging that all of us, to some extent, have been victimized by the professional political classes. Oftentimes in the past, politics brought out the worst in me—much more than I care to admit. Remember, political polarization almost solely benefits the pundits and our two major parties."

My letter concluded by addressing an anonymous reader: "Do you want better government, in which voters and elected officials respect each other? Or do you want to live as plebes in a Democrat or Republican democratically elected autocracy/dictatorship? I can't answer that for you—nor should you want me to answer it for you."

I sent off the email, not sure whether Carl would respond. He did so quickly and graciously.

"I appreciated reading your insights," he wrote. "You capture well the frustration many of us have with the two-party system and the failure to make real tangible progress in a divisive time. The thickness of the animosity between left and right weighs us all down. Sadly, the politicians are always talking past each other."

At the same time, he argued, "there is more commonality among the common voter than what people think…I value your sense of servant leadership that you espouse and the importance of bridge-builders, people willing to listen to both sides, build relationships, and foster new alliances…Rich, I really encourage you to be the community leader you are called to be…Wishing you the best, Carl."

He gave me permission to do what needed to be done. But before I could, I needed to pull out one more brick from that wall.

———◆———

The catalyst came just three days later, in the unexpected form of gun violence.

I had been educating myself about the Second Amendment, and I learned there are more guns than people in the United States. I thought, *If the Democrats are trying to confiscate guns, they're doing a very bad job of it.* I delved deeper into what Democrats were saying about guns. What an eye opener!

In spite of what MAGA said, the Democrats were not coming for our guns. They consistently fought for more gun *regulations* in an attempt to prevent school shootings and other mass murders. But that seemed to be the extent of it. Looking at the issue honestly, I admitted to myself that I had never heard a Democrat call for the confiscation of everyone's weapons.

Next, I researched school shootings. With my newfound open-mindedness, I forced myself to watch interviews with the parents and friends of children who had been gunned down in cold blood. I watched one Republican politician after another prattle on about mental health and hardening school doors. I grew incensed. I also felt a powerful sense of guilt, because I had contributed to this senseless killing by refusing to support reasonable gun restrictions.

> *In spite of what MAGA said, the Democrats were not coming for our guns. They consistently fought for more gun regulations, in an attempt to prevent school shootings and other mass murders.*

Then came May 24. Ironically, that very morning, I had decided to get rid of my AR-15-style semiautomatic rifle. I drove to a pawn shop not far from where I live. As I walked in with my gun, the two owners were glued to the TV on the wall. I joined them and watched in horror as a reporter said a young man had gone on a shooting rampage at Robb Elementary School in Uvalde, Texas, killing nineteen students and two teachers and injuring more than a dozen more. His weapon? An AR-15-style semiautomatic rifle. I looked down at my gun and shuddered.

Like clockwork, Republican politicians and pundits declared the problem was mental health, not guns. I could predict exactly what they would say. I'd been saying the same things since joining MAGA: *We're going to need more guns, not less, to protect our children and society. We need to arm teachers and install better locks and surveillance cameras.*

I was overwhelmed with guilt. I had contributed to this madness. After all those months of sleepless nights wrestling with my conscience, Uvalde crystallized my thinking. I removed the GUNS brick—and the entire wall came crashing down.

To paraphrase Ernest Hemingway, my personal and political epiphany had occurred gradually, and then all at once. I stood in the rubble and realized I was free. I had left MAGA.

PART 3

Life After MAGA
From Isolated Truthteller to a New Purpose and Community

2022-Present

CHAPTER 8

My Loud Apology

My departure from the movement felt a bit anticlimactic. I had already stopped going to pro-Trump events. I'd shut down my podcast and my super PAC. I wasn't hanging out with my MAGA friends anymore. So perhaps it wasn't surprising that no one seemed to miss me. No one came after me. No one asked me why.

But it was a relief. I told a number of non-MAGA friends; I apologized for having deemed them mortal threats to America. When I let Carl know, he said, "I knew you'd come back around to the old Rich!"

I *was* surprised by the growing sense of calm that settled over me. Living in MAGA is much harder than it might seem from the outside. Trump's followers are subjected to nonstop harangues from politicians, pundits, and influencers sowing chaos, fear, and hatred. Seven years of fearmongering had taken a toll on my nervous system. The relentless noise and confusion had traumatized me. My stress level was off the charts.

For the first time in many years, my stress level fell. I could think clearly and make decisions based not on pure emotion, but on logic and facts. Even as citizen Trump kept sowing division and MAGA was as vocal as ever, I no longer dined on their daily doses of anger. I had left the echo chamber. I slept better and took better care of myself.

My improved health allowed me to focus on a new challenge: I had decided what I *didn't* believe, but I was no longer clear on what I *did* believe. When I left MAGA, I didn't suddenly become a Democrat. But I felt confident that I would find my way, now that I was free of Trump's grasp.

> " For the first time in many years, my stress level fell. I could think clearly and make decisions based not on pure emotion, but on logic and facts.

I joined MAGA believing I was part of something that would radically reshape America. It did, although not in a good way. I had been convinced that Trump was the answer to our nation's problems. Admitting I was wrong was extremely painful. But quietly stepping away and notifying some friends felt inadequate. I felt morally compelled to do more.

———◆———

I decided to take public responsibility for the lies I had spread and the damage I had caused while in MAGA. I hadn't been a passive participant. With every article I wrote, every podcast I produced, and every speech I gave, I inflicted another wound on my beloved country.

So I wrote a mea culpa and titled it "The Great Awokening." While leaving MAGA had not necessarily shifted me to the left politically, the progressive group Occupy Democrats agreed to publish my piece on its website. It appeared on August 30, 2022.

To readers surprised to find an essay by "a four-time Donald Trump voter and a two-time Ron DeSantis voter," I explained why I joined MAGA, and how I left it.

"I supported Trump because I believed the fallacy that a Hillary Clinton victory (and, later, a Joe Biden victory) would be the end of America and the start of permanent Democrat rule over our nation," I wrote, noting how my alienation from the two major parties left me open to seeing Trump as a maverick who would shake up the system.

> While leaving MAGA had not necessarily shifted me to the left politically, the progressive group Occupy Democrats agreed to publish my piece on its website. It appeared on August 30, 2022.

During Trump's presidency, "I adopted the right-wing gospel that Democrats were importing foreigners to win elections forever," I said. "Leftists were coming for our guns, nationalism is patriotism, and…a shadowy network of censors" suppressed conservative voices.

I recounted my journey of discovery that led me to quit. "I was wrong about all of it," I wrote, "and acknowledging my errors in judgment was the start of my own personal healing process…I say—with neither a scintilla of hyperbole nor a singular qualm—that Trump is the most politically traumatizing figure in American history."

The "terminally ill" GOP sought to weaken our democracy, I said, arguing that it had "staked a pathway forward that is…backward, with increased emphasis on everything male/Caucasian/Christian and heterosexual."

I predicted that "our nation is about to endure tumult none of us has ever lived through, and the best time to commence healing is right now." Americans needed to conjure "the better and braver angels of our nature…After 246 years of progress, will we cede ground to regression, or will we continue to shape our destiny in the vision of our Founders…?"

The United States "has never run from the fires of threats," I argued. "We run to them with intrepid heroism. There is no obstacle we cannot overcome."

That afternoon, I sat in front of my computer, signed in to Occupy Democrats, and read my article. Going public felt good. I didn't expect much of a response, and that was fine. I wasn't seeking to position myself as some sort of political influencer; I had just followed the dictates of my conscience. But as I lingered over my words, they struck me as inadequate. I started to think that perhaps I *should* play a bigger political role. My mea culpa was all well and good, but one essay on a leftist website would have virtually no impact on the millions of my fellow Americans still in thrall to MAGA. I resolved to do more. But what?

———◆———

I had studiously avoided paying attention back in June 2021 when the House of Representatives created the select committee to investigate January 6; I was still in denial mode. By the time the committee held its first public hearing on June 9, 2022, I had left MAGA and was eager to learn all I could.

I was impressed that, along with seven Democrats, the House had appointed two Republicans—Liz Cheney of Wyoming and Adam Kinzinger of Illinois—to the committee and had made Cheney vice chair. I watched all nine hearings. As involved with MAGA as I'd been, I discovered Trump's deception was much worse than I'd known. I didn't realize the extent to which he had gone to undermine our democratic system, which affirmed that I had made the right decision. Everyone around him knew that what Trump was doing was wrong. They all knew it. And even though I had left MAGA, it was very disappointing to watch Republican House Speaker Kevin McCarthy give the president cover.

The hearings further exposed MAGA's hypocrisy in its supposed support of law enforcement and the rule of law. That support is only forthcoming when it's convenient for the movement.

There had been a time when I would have considered Cheney and Kinzinger as mortal enemies. But of course, that had changed by the time the hearings took place. I considered them quite courageous to go against Trump and their party, although by this time I didn't consider the GOP to be the Republican Party I had grown up with. It was MAGA now.

I had empathy for Cheney and Kinzinger because they were putting their careers on the line, and now had no political home. Rebelling as Republicans against Trump and MAGA put them in a very lonely place. I felt for them and respected them.

———◆———

For the rest of 2022 and until the fall of 2023, I worked in sales for digital products and let the dust settle around my heart and mind. I'd been traumatized while inside of MAGA, and the journey out of the movement had been turbulent and further traumatizing.

Plus, I carried a sense of humiliation. Yes, I was free of the incessant and frantic drumbeat of MAGA pulsing through my life, but I felt like a failure in so many ways. Those few friends I had at that point who had never succumbed to MAGA were happy to see me back, Carl especially. But behind their politeness I detected a tone of derision and disbelief. I knew they could not fathom why or how I had been duped in the first place. How could I explain when I was still trying to figure this out myself? As I struggled with that conundrum, I hit upon the

> I had empathy for Cheney and Kinzinger because they were putting their careers on the line, and now had no political home. Rebelling as Republicans against Trump and MAGA put them in a very lonely place. I felt for them, and respected them.

answer to my question of how I might "do more"—I needed to aggressively spread my story.

With my friends' encouragement, I revised the article posted on Occupy Democrats and published versions on *Salon*, *The New Republic*, and other outlets. I opened Instagram and Twitter accounts and posted about my journey. A few people noticed; some asked for help in talking with friends and family in MAGA. I offered my insights, and that attracted a few more followers.

I wasn't sure if my future held further activism. To be honest, it didn't really appeal to me at that moment. I lay low and let myself heal. Things remained pretty quiet and lonely through the rest of 2022 and into 2023. And then in the fall, my life suddenly changed.

———◆———

In October 2023, I received an email from Paul Glickman, an award-winning retired journalist. He had read a political analysis I wrote for *Daily Kos*, and said, "I am more interested in your personal journey, how you were able to travel from being a MAGA Republican back to living within the real world." He added: "I intend to devote my remaining decades to using my skills to defend democracy and fight for the causes I believe in."

I Googled Paul and learned he had covered the wars in Central America in the 1980s, served as a foreign editor at NPR in the '90s, and was news director at a large Los Angeles radio station for many years after that. I was humbled and excited. I thought, "Wow, this is a really serious person who wants to work with me!" It gave me hope that maybe, just maybe, I really could make amends for the damage I'd caused and help other people leave MAGA.

I quickly wrote back: "Perhaps we could collaborate. I'm sure our civic interests align. Let's do a Zoom call!" During our call, I told him the phrase "Leaving MAGA" kept popping into my head, and that it seemed like the perfect name for a nonprofit organization. I said that with a nonprofit, we could create a website and post testimonials of other people who had left MAGA. Paul thought that was a great idea and said, "I would love to help."

I had never worked in the nonprofit world, so I didn't have the faintest idea where to start. I did know my guiding principle was that the nonprofit would be nonpartisan. When I left MAGA, I didn't switch from Republican to Democrat. I did not want to become a recruitment center for the Democratic Party. I wanted to offer a safe, non-judgmental space for people who were having doubts or questions about MAGA, to help them deal with the trauma they experienced, and to hopefully help them through the process of leaving.

———◆———

Just two weeks after Paul reached out, my nonprofit dream took a huge step toward reality. I attended a "Democracy Summit" at Howard University in Washington, DC, hosted by the school's Center for Journalism & Democracy. I learned about the event because I had been following Nikole Hannah-Jones, the Center's founder and the creator and lead author of *The 1619 Project*, a book that had a profound impact on me. The Democracy Summit was only open to journalists and researchers, but it also offered scholarships. I applied, and to my surprise I was accepted.

The event explored how to better report on threats to democracy. The journalist Joy Reid moderated one panel that included Nadine Smith, executive director of the LGBTQ+ rights group Equality Florida, and nonprofit veteran Lia Gaines, past president of the NAACP chapter in West Palm Beach, Florida. I had met Lia that morning, because we ended up sharing an Uber from our hotel to the conference site. I grabbed a front row seat, and when it was time for questions, I stood up, introduced myself and explained that I wanted to help people leave MAGA.

After the session, Nadine caught up with me in the hallway. She said, "Once we both get back to Florida, I'd like to talk with you more about how we might work together."

I said, "That would be great. I have this idea about starting a nonprofit, but I have no idea what's involved."

She said, "I can help with that!"

Lia and I had exchanged numbers, and when I got back home, I called her and laid out my plan. "That's great, we need something like that," she said, and immediately offered to lend a hand.

Suddenly, I had a team. Nadine and Lia shepherded me through the rigorous nonprofit application process. Without their help, I would have had to spend thousands of dollars on attorney fees. I had the funds to hire a web developer, thanks to Leaving MAGA's first financial backer, startup investor Christopher Deutsch. A friend of Paul's connected us with Keith Knueven, owner of a graphic design firm in Los Angeles. He agreed to create a logo pro bono. I loved what he came up with: two overlapping circles—one red, one blue, both with white striation. Keith said he wanted an image that symbolized unity.

Meanwhile, Paul oversaw and edited website content. He also worked with me to develop the all-important mission statement:

- Empower people to leave MAGA and tell their stories
- Foster reconciliation with friends and family
- Develop movement leaders to help others leave

IRS approval of our nonprofit status would come a few months later, but we incorporated Leaving MAGA in January 2024. We were official!

CHAPTER 9

A New Life After MAGA

On January 23, 2024, I checked my Twitter account. Even though I was active on it, I had very few followers. But on that day, the number of my followers skyrocketed. I knew that someone with a big following must have engaged with something I wrote, so I went back into my tweets to find the source. To my surprised delight, Adam Kinzinger had re-tweeted my "Great Awokening" article. I wrote to him privately on Twitter and we soon connected on Zoom. I was so grateful for his support. After that, we stayed connected and became friends.

Fast forward to the summer of 2024. Adam approached me and said, "Hey, would you like an introduction to the Biden campaign?"

I said, "Sure, absolutely!" The next thing I knew, I was on a Zoom call with Jen O'Malley Dillon, President Biden's national campaign chair. We talked about what role I might play.

Afterward, I reflected on the astonishingly long distance I had traveled. After spending several years as a hardcore MAGA pundit trashing everyone in the Democratic Party as evil traitors, here I was, in a private meeting with the woman running Biden's national campaign!

I wasn't jumping on board blindly. After I left MAGA, I researched what the Democratic Party actually believes, and what I learned impressed me. I might disagree with the party in certain areas, but it is motivated by a desire to expand rights and to provide everyone with decent jobs, housing, good schools, clean air, and affordable health care. Compared with Trump and MAGA's authoritarian agenda built on a foundation of lies, the choice was easy.

Not one week after my meeting with Biden's team, his disastrous debate performance against Trump brought any possible collaboration with me to a crashing halt. But then Biden dropped out of the race about a month later and endorsed Vice President Kamala Harris. She kept most of his top campaign officials, including Dillon. So I decided to reach out again.

———◆———

A few weeks later, I found myself traveling to Miami to record a speech that would be played at the Democratic National Convention in Chicago. By this time, I was a Florida co-chair of Republicans for Harris. I had asked the campaign if I could address the convention live, but they didn't have room for me in the lineup. They said I could record a one-minute video.

I arrived at the campaign office carrying a hanger that held the clothes I'd wear on camera. I expected to find a couple of staffers with a small video setup.

I swung open the door and, to my surprise, about a dozen people buzzed around the room. They showed me to the bathroom so I could change, and before I knew it, I was nervously sitting in front of the camera, with everyone watching me and convention organizers in Chicago listening in remotely.

We rehearsed my lines, and then it was showtime. On the first take, I was a bit awkward, so we needed to do a second one. Then a third. On the fourth take, I nailed it.

The campaign played the video on the first night of the convention. As thousands of people in the United Center (and many more on C-SPAN) watched me on the jumbotron, I said that when I left MAGA I learned that Trump "had been lying about pretty much everything. Lying is Trump's toxic superpower. He's ripped apart families, communities—our whole country. So this is my message to all the Republicans and independents who are watching—people like me who voted for and believed in Trump: I made a grave mistake, but it's never too late to change your mind. You don't need to agree with everything you hear tonight to do what is right. We need to be able to trust our leaders; that's why I'm all in for Kamala Harris."

> I said that when I left MAGA I learned that Trump "had been lying about pretty much everything. Lying is Trump's toxic superpower. He's ripped apart families, communities— our whole country."

It was a heady moment. My speech sparked a flurry of media interest. CNN interviewed me, and MSNBC had me on twice. *The New York Times*, *USA Today*, NPR, the *Miami Herald*, the *Chicago Sun-Times*, Sirius XM, *Rolling Stone*, and other outlets interviewed me. Then I got to meet the candidate.

On October 16, I flew to Philadelphia to attend a Republicans for Harris rally at Washington Crossing Historic Park, near the site of George Washington's famous crossing of the Delaware in the Revolutionary War. More than 100 Republican luminaries—including former members of Congress and former state officials—had gathered for the event. We filed into a theater to wait for the rally to begin. I felt the same way I did at the banquet I had attended at Mar-a-Lago four years earlier—intoxicated by the excitement of a presidential campaign.

I found Adam Kinzinger; it was the first time we met face-to-face. We shook hands, and I said, "I want to thank you for supporting Leaving MAGA and giving me the opportunity to do what I can to push back."

"Hey, man," he said, "you have an important story to tell, and I'm happy to help."

An aide led me over to meet Vice President Harris. I told her of my interest in working to foster national reconciliation between MAGA supporters and their opponents after she won the election. She loved the idea and thanked me for my contributions.

The rally was thrilling. Harris appeared on stage with many high-profile Republicans, including Adam, Bill Kristol and former Congressman Denver Riggleman.

The day gave me a jolt of adrenalin; the show of Republican support for the Democrat led me to think Harris could win. And if she did, I would have a chance to atone for all the damage I'd caused while in MAGA.

I knew that, regardless of the outcome of the election, Leaving MAGA's work would continue. Either way, millions would remain in Trump's thrall. When he defeated Harris on November 5, I was devastated for the country. Those of us who had been paying attention knew he intended to undermine our democracy. We pressed on with our work.

———◆———

Today, Leaving MAGA has never been busier. We're publishing a growing number of testimonials by people who left the movement. I have been invited to speak at numerous events around the country. I drove a mobile billboard to Mar-a-Lago and parked it outside the resort. Supporters used their own money to erect Leaving MAGA billboards in Pennsylvania and Tennessee. We've garnered more media attention; *The New Yorker Radio Hour* interviewed me, as did MS NOW's Stephanie Ruhle and Nicolle Wallace. Swedish, German, and Japanese outlets have all produced stories about me.

In the summer of 2025, I got the idea of starting a support group for people with friends and family in MAGA. A colleague introduced me to Julianna Forlano, a social worker and therapist. She eagerly agreed to lead the group. Juliana had a vision: help people heal from the harm caused by those strained relationships, in part by processing their frustration and feelings of betrayal.

"At the same time, it's important that they understand it's not their responsibility to change their loved one or convince them to leave MAGA," she said in one of our phone calls. Juliana developed an ongoing series of weekly Zoom sessions, each with its own theme, ranging from "Grief, Loss, and Letting Go: Transforming Our Losses" to "Reclaiming Your Inner Authority: Ending the Vigilance Loop."

We launched the first support group in October 2025, and as of February 2026 it is still going strong. On average, about forty people attend. The sessions are emotional rollercoasters. Participants pour out their fury, despair, and sadness. There are also plenty of moments of hopefulness and clarity. Dozens of them have emailed me expressing their gratitude. "I didn't know how alone I felt until I walked into this group," wrote one. "Being with other people going through the same thing has been deeply healing." Another said: "I've done 12-step. I've done recovery circles. I've done narcissistic abuse work. This is Al-Anon for families of MAGA. It's exactly what I need." And another wrote: "I don't spiral after family interactions anymore. I actually have tools now."

So, Leaving MAGA is thriving. Nothing will deter us from our mission. Our purpose is clear. And in the face of Donald Trump's escalating outrages, I am more certain every day that we are on the right path.

I have learned so much from those who joined Leaving MAGA. For example, there is no stereotypical MAGA American; they come from all walks of life and each person has a unique story.

We know certain factors come into play across the board. For instance, MAGA isolates its followers from anyone who challenges the dogma, and dehumanizes its opponents. That's why the information feedback loop plays such a critical role in keeping the masses faithful.

But for many, the cascade of lies becomes unbearable, and the promises fall horribly short of expectations. Disappointment replaces certainty, and a sense of betrayal takes hold. The cracks in the wall widen as a person opens up to outside sources of information. Leaving MAGA is rarely a quick or easy process. It requires admitting to a serious mistake and walking away from one's community.

When the wall finally crashes, people can feel disoriented and alone. That's one of the reasons I founded Leaving MAGA—to show there are many ready to walk alongside those who quit the movement.

The next section presents the true stories of six people who enthusiastically joined MAGA only to discover later on that they had taken a wrong turn, and that they needed to get out. Their journeys—like mine— demonstrate that there is, indeed, life after MAGA.

PART 4

Stories from Leaving MAGA

From Betrayal to Healing

———•———

CHAPTER 10

Stephania Messina

Accountability Without Self-destruction

I'm back to myself with a faith stripped of fear.

Stephania Messina was born in 1985 in Philadelphia into a "big, crazy, loud Greek-Italian family." Her parents moved to Detroit shortly before her fifth birthday. She remembers a chaotic household; her father was a heroin addict, prompting many fights with her mother. While Stephania knew her parents were Democrats, they really didn't discuss politics.

I think there's a disconnect from politics when you're working just to get enough food on the table, while making sure your husband isn't taking money for drugs.

Church played a big role in her early years. *Throughout my childhood, we attended an Assemblies of God church, complete with speaking in tongues and gifts of the Spirit. We left when I was about nine after it emerged that the pastor had embezzled a lot of money. By my teen years, I wasn't religious, although I believed in God.*

Stephania was determined to get a good education. *School was everything to me. I wanted to be the first in my family to go to college. Meanwhile, I had long battled anxiety, along with undiagnosed ADHD. After I graduated from high school, I enrolled at Wayne State University. But panic attacks brought on by my ADHD made me feel like an impostor. I dropped out.*

Pre-MAGA Influences

She got pregnant at nineteen. When her son Zak was two, Stephania discovered his father Gary was addicted to pills. She had vowed never to be with an addict, so she left him, moved back in with her parents, and returned to college.

She met her husband Dan in 2009. His experiences shaped her political outlook. *He had served three years in the Air Force, and smoked marijuana for severe knee pain. We really got into Ron Paul, who was pro-decriminalization. We also watched Joe Rogan's early stuff, since he also was staunchly pro-decriminalization.*

Stephania completed her Associate Degree in Applied Science in 2010 and started working as a respiratory therapist in the NICU in the University of Michigan's Children's Hospital, a job she loved. Meanwhile, she and her husband became committed political independents.

Dan had a few close friends in the Army who deployed to Afghanistan and were never the same. One came home with severe PTSD. That really informed our politics; I had voted for Barack Obama in 2008 because I wanted a change after the George W. Bush administration's lies about weapons of mass destruction. Now we felt Obama had betrayed us by staying in Afghanistan. We both voted for Ron Paul in 2012.

The couple endured severe financial struggles over the next couple of years and had to move into a small apartment. *I struggled mightily with depression. I started praying. I reached out to God, read the Bible. In September 2014, I had a spiritual awakening. I felt I was saved. I didn't realize it, but that was the moment that set me on my journey toward MAGA.*

Stepania had little time for politics when Trump ran for president the first time. She was suffering from severe postpartum depression after the birth of her fourth son, and her dad had just been diagnosed with cancer (he passed away that December). In any event, the 2016 candidates did not excite her. *I didn't like Trump or Hillary Clinton, and I felt my vote didn't matter.*

A scandal in Stephania's evangelical Assemblies of God church accelerated her political transformation. *We switched to a charismatic church with fewer than 50 people in the congregation. It was there I became extremely fundamentalist. The pastor was preaching an interpretation of the Bible that I realized much later was Christian Nationalist.*

Joining the MAGA Movement

By the summer of 2017, Stephania's religious conversion had her primed to enthusiastically join MAGA. *I had come to believe America is a Christian nation, and it was always meant to be. We were taught the world belongs to Satan, so there would always be people trying to make the US less Christian. We were most worked up about Roe v. Wade and gay marriage. We believed we wouldn't have blessings on our land until we got rid of those things.*

Religion merged with politics. *It was critical to have a president who would carry out this agenda. It could have been anyone, as long as they were willing to carry out the Christian Nationalist agenda. It happened to be Trump. We were thrilled with Trump's Supreme Court picks. He promised evangelicals this would be the end of legalized abortion. In our church, the women were told to be a Quiverfull Christian. You wanted to point in the direction of the Lord, and your kids were the arrows in your quiver. We were praised when we had lots of kids; it was intoxicating.*

Stephania loved that Trump prioritized America and promised to bring back jobs from China. *We excused or explained away his philandering and controversial remarks. The church told us he had been chosen by God, that he was a disheveled man like David, who also was an adulterer. Trump was a "baby Christian," meaning he had just gotten saved, so we should give him grace because we're all sinners. Since he was a new creature in Christ, you couldn't hold anything against him.*

There was nothing anyone could say to shake her from her convictions. *We believed Trump's critics were just blinded by Satan. We saw him as the persecuted white savior, fighting for us. I was MAGA all the way, but I didn't know it meant Make America Great Again. To us, MAGA meant Make America Godly Again.*

Stephania settled into an insular information bubble. *I relied almost entirely on conservative Christian pastors for my information. I read Focus on the Family's publication. I watched Fox News and listened to a local Christian radio host who was 100 percent pro-Trump.*

Cracks in the MAGA Wall

Despite her Christian Nationalist devotion to MAGA, Stephania knew deep down that the person she had become did not match who she had once been. *All the while, I was suppressing major internal turmoil. On the outside, I was this sage Christian, the meek and quiet wife who home-schooled the kids and stood behind her man, never calling attention to myself. But I had been a feminist before my religious awakening, and that created so much cognitive dissonance that I was in constant mental anguish.*

> " MAGA meant Make America Godly Again.

Stephania let the pastor's wife mentor her, a move she soon regretted. *I emulated her authoritarian homeschooling approach, which included hitting and spanking. My relationships with my boys suffered. I was racked with guilt.*

Cracks also appeared in her marriage. *In our pre-church life, Dan and I had been best friends, doing everything together. But we became the kind of couple the church told us we had to be. It almost tore us apart, although I never discussed any of my internal anguish with Dan.*

With the onset of the pandemic, Stephania found herself torn between her religious beliefs and her knowledge of respiratory infections. *When COVID hit in 2020, I believed it was a demonic Democrat ploy to shut down churches. Our church kept meeting in person, even though we weren't supposed to. As a medical professional, I realized that because of the insular nature of our community—the moms were all at home and the dads worked with each other—that we had created the kind of "pod" that public health experts said was a safe place for people to congregate. So we were shielded from the pandemic's impacts, which made us very insensitive to what was happening.*

Her congregation saw COVID as apocalyptic. *We came to believe the pandemic was a sign of the end times, that it would bring about the second coming of Christ.* But she couldn't ignore the public health issues. *I also saw that when it came to the vaccine, Trump talked out of both sides of his mouth: He praised it and took credit for it, while at the same time he downplayed the effects of COVID and said, "Don't get vaccinated." But you couldn't criticize him.*

Every church in the area was anti-vax and anti-mask. *But with my medical training, I understood the devastating effects of upper respiratory illness, and that masks stopped transmission. I started to see hypocrisy: we were loving Christians, striving to protect those around us. But people were dying. Our church became even more Christian Nationalist. The thinking was, in a Christian nation, you can't force people to get vaccinated, we have free will. That struck me as convoluted reasoning that was neither Christian nor patriotic.*

One Betrayal Too Many

Around the same time, friends introduced Stephania to QAnon, and she fell for it hard. *When Trump claimed the 2020 election was stolen, I wholeheartedly believed him. We believed Jan. 6 was the day—as Q predicted—that Trump would claim his rightful place as president and expose the evil cabal of child-eating, adrenochrome-taking Democrats operating under a pizza parlor in Washington.*

Then it didn't happen. We watched as the goal posts kept moving. Every time Trump would do something, QAnon people on Parlor would say: "This is it, this is the time." They predicted a massive shutdown of the electrical grid. Then nothing. After several weeks of this, I realized, "You're getting played."

The death of her son Zak's father in a March 2021 motorcycle accident shook Stephania to the core, and destroyed her relationship with her church. *At Gary's funeral, the pastor's wife told Zak it was probably a good thing his dad had died, that he was probably better off because Gary wasn't a Christian and he wasn't around to influence him. My best friend basically told me the same thing. These people I considered close family, brothers and sisters in Christ, were telling my son he was better off without his dad. I was reaching the end of my rope.*

Two months later, Dan threw out his back, and they missed church for six weeks. *During that time, I discussed everything I hadn't been telling him, and we never went back. We were called apostates, heretics. They said we were fakes who were never really for them, that it was all an act.*

In September 2021, Dan got long COVID and couldn't work for months. *Meanwhile, I finally got diagnosed with ADHD. I had been getting help with my mental health, and the diagnosis helped bring my time in MAGA into perspective. I finally realized I wasn't crazy.*

We started our deconstruction of the religion at this time. That process exposed the reality that large chunks of the American church had been captured by Christian Nationalism—a political ideology disguised as theology. That was when I left MAGA.

Expanding News Sources

Stephania began to search out other perspectives and seek the information she had been told would harm her. *When the veil dropped, it dropped hard. I jumped on TikTok, and learned there was an ex-evangelical movement out there. That helped me a lot. I started reading books other than the Bible again. I read about psychology and trauma, trying to wrap my head around what had happened to me.*

... large chunks of the American church had been captured by Christian Nationalism— a political ideology disguised as theology. That was when I left MAGA.

After being a faithful follower of *One America News* and *NewsMax*, she switched to NPR. *I had been taught that outside media was corrupt and dangerous. Once I allowed myself to look again—to read, listen, and learn—the scale of my ignorance became clear. I had voted to strip others of rights while believing I was being righteous. That realization was devastating. I believe in doing no harm, and I had done harm. I started doing real research. I started to think critically again. In the church and MAGA I was not thinking for myself.*

Stephania's research into COVID angered her. *So many people focus on Jan. 6 as Trump's worst moment, but I think his lack of leadership during COVID was one of the most egregious acts of any president.*

I did a lot of intense work undoing my internalized misogyny, which had been reinforced by Trump and the church. I also returned to my old pro-choice position. When I was 14, my best friend got an abortion, and after that I felt, "Who am I to play God in someone else's major life decisions?" And yet as a Christian Nationalist, I became vehemently anti-choice. It's amazing the things you will believe to conform to groupthink.

> " I believe in doing no harm, and I had done harm. I started doing real research. I started to think critically again. In the church and MAGA I was not thinking for myself.

Building a New Life—and a New Community

In March 2022, Stephania returned to work at the children's hospital where she had worked previously. She watched administrators cut corners to save money, while cleanliness and staffing shortages put children at risk. She learned the CEO received large bonuses. Stephania found the situation intolerable, and quit.

I next got a job taking care of a billionaire with a severe disease that kept her homebound. She had a day and night nurse manager, a staff nurse, a home health aide, me as her respiratory therapist, and a maid. The injustice of it all over- whelmed me: The wealthy can get what they need while working-class people struggle to survive.

The more I learned, the more I found myself moving hard left. I considered Democrats to be the new right, and Republicans to just be off the map entirely, fascists who don't deserve a place in our democracy.

Stephania has found religious peace. *Today I feel more spiritually fulfilled than ever. I'm seeing Jesus clearly, and seeing the way fundamentalism has destroyed the good news of the Gospel. God loves us all, understands our suffering, and wants us to love and support one another with empathy and without prideful judgment.*

Now that I'm critically thinking again, I ask myself, what did Jesus do? He was homeless; he sat with the "sin- ners." Looking at Jesus through sober eyes free from the in- toxication of the church has led me to be a more authentic Christian, as I seek to love and support others without the bigotry and hate that fundamentalists in MAGA falsely be- lieve is God's way, and that they use to justify their support of Trump.

She has discarded a lot of damaging lessons. *Leaving MAGA required accountability without self-destruction. Through therapy and education, I began unlearning inter- nalized patriarchy, racism, and class mythology. I became a feminist again because I understood how deeply submission had been demanded of me. I became antiracist because I saw how fear had been taught to me as instinct. I learned to forgive myself while refusing to excuse my past choices.*

Stephania is now working part-time as a pediatric respiratory therapist, but she considers her most important work to be at home. *We are raising five young white boys to reject the ideology we once taught them. We are not raising Christian nationalists or white supremacists or billionaire bootlickers. We're raising empathetic, emotionally intelligent children, so they will understand and have core values for justice, intersectionality, and the responsibility of privilege. Leaving MAGA brought me back to myself—to my faith stripped of fear, and to a moral clarity rooted not in obedience, but in evidence, compassion, and action.*

Joining Leaving MAGA provided the community Stephania needed. *Finding the Leaving MAGA movement showed me that my story was not unique. Again and again, I encountered people who had entered MAGA through parallel pathways—churches, algorithmic media, grievance-based identity—each believing they were acting in good faith. Recognizing those patterns transformed my anger into purpose.*

> Leaving MAGA brought me back to myself—to my faith stripped of fear, and to a moral clarity rooted not in obedience, but in evidence, compassion, and action.

What unites us is not a desire for absolution, but a commitment to accountability. Naming indoctrination does not excuse harm—it explains it so it can be prevented. That distinction matters. The hard part about leaving MAGA isn't changing your mind; it's deciding what you're willing to lose afterward—community, family, identity. This movement understands that cost.

She wholeheartedly endorses the strategy of reaching out with compassion to people in MAGA. *I advocate for empathy as a strategy. Not everyone deserves engagement, but many people do—especially those we love who have been indoctrinated. Humiliation entrenches extremism; connection disrupts it. I've seen this work firsthand.*

Speaking out publicly has helped Stephania navigate political estrangement within her family. *Relationships I once believed were lost have been repaired. My own brother no longer supports Trump. He credits our conversations with helping him realize his information ecosystem was a right-wing echo chamber. My efforts don't always have the intended effect; other family members have remained staunchly in support of the Trump regime.*

The Leaving MAGA movement has also given my voice reach I never expected—from academic research abroad to media projects on political dissent. But the most meaningful impact has been the messages from people who tell me my story helped them choose understanding over estrangement. The right mobilizes fear. We mobilize hope. We stand against unjust power, refuse dehumanization, and insist that people are more than the worst ideology they were taught. Leaving MAGA helped give me my agency back. Joining this movement helped give that agency direction.

For more of Stephania's story.

CHAPTER 11
Steve Vilchez
No Longer Living in Fear

I came to realize that I had made a mistake.

Steve Vilchez was born in 2003 and grew up in the Chicago suburb of Berwyn. For someone who joined MAGA, he has an unusual background.

My mom worked on the assembly line for a manufacturing company; my dad was a manager for a company that made products for the construction industry. My parents—both undocumented Mexican immigrants—never talked politics at home. They watched the local Spanish TV news channel, which was more interested in local crime stories than serious political coverage.

Steve became interested in politics during the 2016 elections, just two months shy of his thirteenth birthday. *We held a mock election in one of my classes a few weeks before Election Day—Hillary Clinton won 94 percent and Donald*

Trump won 3 percent. Election night fascinated me; I had 50 tabs open on my iPad, tracking every state's results.

Steve went to sleep thinking Clinton would win. *When it turned out Trump won, I was very surprised and nervous, because there had been a lot of fearmongering about what he would do.*

Despite Trump's harsh rhetoric about people like his parents, he decided to begin listening to more conservative news. *When Trump won the election, I told myself to be open-minded. To my nearly 13-year-old brain, being open-minded didn't mean listening to both sides; it meant I should reject what I used to listen to and start listening to Trump and his supporters.*

Up until that point Steve had gotten his news from CNN, MSNBC, Vice, Vox, and left-leaning commentators. *I stopped following all of them. My sources of information became Fox (I particularly liked Tucker Carlson), Newsmax, OAN, the Daily Wire, Breitbart, Candace Owens, Ben Shapiro, Charlie Kirk—anything or anyone who claimed to be pro-Trump and America First. I started listening to Alex Jones's InfoWars. I completely trusted what he said.*

Joining the MAGA Movement

Steve jumped in with gusto. *I became a full-throated MAGA American. I was probably one of the youngest people ever to join.* Though he disagreed with many things Trump said—specifically related to climate and vaccine science—he kept those thoughts to himself.

I was very pro-Trump. I embraced anything Trump said. I also became a bundle of contradictions. I backed

Trump's call to build a border wall paid for by Mexico, despite both my parents being undocumented. I even thought we should send troops to shoot people trying to cross illegally into the US.

Steve never had an explanation for his contradictions. *I told myself it made sense to do what Trump wanted while finding a way to protect my mom from his policies. (I was living with my mom by that point; my parents separated a few weeks after Trump took office in 2017.)*

Joining MAGA led me to shift my moral compass. Before the 2016 election, I was very upset by Trump's comment about grabbing women by the pussy. But once I joined MAGA, I defended him. I parroted what he said, it was just locker room talk.

He became more outspoken in high school about being a proud MAGA member. Friends he'd known for a long time stopped talking to him. Then COVID swept the country.

When the pandemic hit, my internal contradictions were in full flower. I bought into Trump's COVID agenda and strongly supported Operation Warp Speed. But I became an opponent of the vaccine. I had been fed a nonstop stream of stories from pro-MAGA accounts that Bill Gates was behind the vaccine and had implanted a microchip in it that would track all sorts of information about a person. There was a

> " I was very pro-Trump. I embraced anything Trump said. I also became a bundle of contradictions. I backed Trump's call to build a border wall paid for by Mexico, despite both my parents being undocumented.

steady drumbeat of accusations that Gates was evil, working for the Deep State.

Steve had his doubts about some of the conspiracy theories. *I wasn't fully convinced by the microchip theory, but I was conditioned to distrust Gates, so I thought something suspicious was going on. I never knew he was just funding vaccine research and development.*

Cracks in the MAGA Wall

The contradictions began to pile up. Steve recoiled when Trump suggested people might fight off COVID by injecting bleach or shining a light through their body. *I'm a big believer in science, so I knew those things weren't true.*

There was more. *Trump's "shithole countries" comment made me raise an eyebrow. I was also disturbed by Trump's claim that climate change is a hoax. I knew there were thousands of years of data proving it's real. But I was so deep into MAGA that I went along with what he said, at least outwardly. Privately, I knew he was wrong.*

Steve was confident Trump would be elected in 2020. *I wasn't prepared for what happened. When Fox News called Arizona for Biden, I was stunned. Then I saw Rudy Giuliani claiming there was fraud. I thought, no way Biden won Arizona, there must have been some fraud. I had the same reaction with regard to North Carolina and Georgia, since the early returns had Trump ahead. I went into full election denialism; I was convinced the presidency had been stolen from Donald Trump.*

Although every recount and audit, along with virtually every court case, confirmed that Biden had won, Steve held firm. *I refused to believe it. I thought it was a bunch of BS. I figured that all the Republican election officials and Trump-appointed judges had faked their loyalty to Trump to get their jobs, and now that they had them, they were showing their true colors.*

At the same time, Trump's incessant claims about election fraud widened the cracks in Steve's wall. *While I still believed him, the thought did enter my mind: "What if it wasn't stolen and he's just saying it was stolen?" But I suppressed the thought.*

Everything changed for Steve on January 6. *I was in my 11th grade English class when Trump supporters breached the police lines and entered the building. My teacher canceled class and we all watched the live coverage. I was speechless. I couldn't think of anything to defend Trump on this. It made me question whether he was a great man, because for the most part he let it happen.*

The day's events left Steve angry. *I felt Republicans should be ashamed of themselves. We're a democracy and we should fight to continue being a democracy. That was one of the first moments when I began to question my allegiance to MAGA.*

One Betrayal Too Many

Steve stayed in MAGA, but January 6 led him to diversify his news providers. *A few months later I decided I needed to become truly open-minded. I was now 17, and I understood by then that to be open-minded means getting information from a variety of sources. I continued listening to my right-wing outlets, although not as much. I stopped listening to*

InfoWars because it was too far right for me. I went back to CNN and NBC, and found a lot of insightful coverage.

Steve stuck with Trump, but felt the ground moving under his feet. *I found myself shifting to the left, particularly on immigration and health care. I tried to look at things from the standpoint of morality. I mean, these are human beings we're talking about. For example, my parents are very low-income, but they should have the same access to health care as anyone else. So I embraced Obamacare.*

Then he shifted left on gun control, LGBTQ+ rights, and taxes. *I was a big proponent of tax cuts but now I'm more a backer of a progressive tax, because if the rich paid more taxes we could use it for public services. And yet I still backed MAGA and Trump!*

The last straw for Steve was the 2022 midterm elections. *Trump endorsed so many election deniers, like Kari Lake, who ran for governor of Arizona, and Bobby Piton, who ran for US Senate in Illinois. When they lost, they again claimed fraud. After what happened on January 6, I knew we couldn't have that happen again. That was it—I was done with MAGA.*

Nowadays, he's preoccupied with how Trump's mass deportation campaign might affect his family. *During the ICE raids in the Chicagoland area, I was calling my mom twice a day, before and after she went to work, just to make sure she wasn't taken. A couple months ago, ICE agents raided the daycare center in Chicago where my mom drops off the kids she babysits. They showed up an hour after she had left. Another time, ICE was on my street when my mom was visiting me.*

Steve has frequent conversations with his mother about what they'll do if ICE takes her and breaks up their family. *Mom applied for a green card three times but was rejected each time. Because of Trump, until noon on January 20, 2029, there could come a day when I call her and she doesn't answer, because she's been*

> **" "** After what happened on January 6, I knew we couldn't have that happen again. That was it—I was done with MAGA.

taken by ICE. Again, it's about morality. We're all human beings; we deserve not to be treated as criminals just because we're seeking a better life in the US.

He has almost entirely stopped following MAGA media. *I cut off Newsmax, OAN, Tucker Carlson, Candace Owens, Steve Bannon, and anyone else whose motto is, "Trump good." I now get a lot of my political information from ABC, CNN, NBC, MS NOW, and left-leaning activists like Harry Sisson. I still check out Fox to see what they're saying about what's going on.*

I'm mystified at how evangelicals support Trump. I don't understand what they actually believe in. And things have gone too far with Christian Nationalism. When Trump started selling Trump-endorsed Bibles, I thought, "Jesus would not like that at all."

Building a New Life—and a New Community

Steve carries the wisdom of his story with him. He's in his last year at Illinois State University, completing a degree in Biology Teacher Education. He wants to teach high school science and is thankful for all the changes leaving MAGA has brought in his life.

I've learned a lot about myself in college. When I left high school, I was a pompous ass. Then I discovered most everyone at college was smarter than me. That opened my horizon to new perspectives, to understanding that everyone, including LGBTQ+, underprivileged, and marginalized people, are just seeking basic rights. I saw that MAGA wants to strip away their rights. If you had told me six years ago that I would be a supporter of LGBTQ+ rights, I would have called you a bunch of nasty names.

Leaving the MAGA movement has been rejuvenating. When I was in it, I always felt as if I was living in fear of the unknown. Now I feel a whole lot better about myself, knowing I can disagree with someone without fear. I love civil debate. I love asking questions. That's why I want to be a teacher, to help answer my students' questions.

Steve feels intellectually liberated. *I'm much more of a free thinker now. I no longer have to worry about whether what I think or believe is contrary to what Trump thinks. I now consider myself part of the Bernie Sanders/AOC wing of the Democratic Party.*

He has had mixed results when sharing his story with others. *I told some of my new friends in college about my political experience and they were OK with it. Sadly, most of my friends who had stopped talking to me did not resume our relationships after I left MAGA. A couple of old high school friends put up with whatever nonsense I said throughout my MAGA period, and we're still close.*

Steve has found a place to belong in Leaving MAGA, and feels he is learning valuable lessons. *The Leaving MAGA organization has taught me a lot. We're not seeking vengeance—we want to understand why people are in MAGA, to know them as people and treat them with respect. If you treat people with respect, they're going to respect you.*

He relishes his role as a truthteller. *I love that Leaving MAGA provides an opportunity to educate people. I'm happy that I've been able to publicly share my story, which is something I rarely do in my day-to-day life. Most of the people who have reached out to me have been positive. Occasionally someone says, "Why were you in MAGA in the first place? You should have known better." But I was 13, I didn't know anything about life. At least I came to realize that I had made a mistake.*

> *The Leaving MAGA organization has taught me a lot. We're not seeking vengeance—we want to understand why people are in MAGA, to know them as people and treat them with respect.*

Telling our stories lets others in MAGA know we exist, that just because you're in the movement, it doesn't mean you have to stay in it forever. I'm sure a lot of people have quietly left MAGA but are too scared to go public. Knowing that someone might read my story and get inspired to think, "Maybe I need to leave MAGA too," that just makes me want to keep going with this work.

For more of Steve's story.

CHAPTER 12
Bailee Tyler
Finding a Safe Community

I can share my story without judgment.

Bailee Tyler was born in 1996 and raised in Cherryvale, a small, struggling rural town in southeast Kansas. Cherryvale was the kind of town where *everyone knew everyone*. It was surrounded by cows and cornfields—and marked by poverty and addiction.

Her family struggled with both poverty and addiction. *My dad made good money, but he was a meth addict, so he spent all our money on drugs. We lived in an old trailer in the middle of nowhere.*

Her parents weren't deeply religious, but church still played a role in her childhood. Occasionally her family attended a non-denominational church in a nearby town, and Bailee went to Vacation Bible School—a formative experience that left a lasting impression. *I became a conservative Christian, and that made me strongly anti-abortion.*

Her parents didn't discuss politics much at home. The news was rarely on. But like many kids growing up in conservative Christian environments, her worldview was shaped quietly and powerfully by the culture around her—church, community, and the voices she trusted.

Barack Obama was president during Bailee's middle and high school years, and her political awareness was simple and inherited: *All I knew was that everyone disliked him, so I did too.*

Joining the MAGA Movement

Bailee was twenty when Donald Trump ran for president in 2016. Along with those who were influential in her life, she voted for Trump. But her vote didn't indicate that she saw herself as part of the MAGA movement. *I wasn't political. I wasn't educated. I had heard a few things about Trump that appealed to me—he talked about improving the economy, and he ran on an anti-abortion platform.*

Once Trump was president, however, Bailee became more interested in politics, and in 2018 she began listening to conservative media figures like Ben Shapiro, Matt Walsh, Joe Rogan, and Megyn Kelly. They became her primary sources of information—and they reinforced everything she already believed.

Bailee made the decision that most MAGA followers make: to eliminate all sources of information other than those that unquestioningly support the movement. For two years, she lived inside a sealed information bubble, shutting out anything that challenged her worldview. Cut off from the larger political conversation in the country, she fell prey to MAGA's agenda.

I wasn't willing to see different perspectives. They validated me and I became a full-blown MAGA supporter. I got really angry, and I started a lot of arguments with people over politics—even though I couldn't really back up what I was saying. I just repeated what I'd heard. I felt like I knew everything. I didn't care about others.

Cracks in the MAGA Wall

Over the next couple of years, several events converged to crack the walls that had kept Bailee in MAGA. First, in 2019, she enrolled at the online University of Southern Mississippi to pursue a degree in Industrial Engineering. That seemingly nonpolitical act had a profound impact on her life. *I learned how to think critically, conduct research, and verify information. That opened my eyes and changed my worldview.*

That awakening led Bailee to intensively reexamine her faith. She still believed in Jesus, but she started peppering church leaders with difficult questions, *and they either couldn't answer or gave answers that didn't make sense.* She married a man in 2020 who didn't share her religious beliefs, which prompted her to ask a particularly tough question: *Would my husband—an atheist—go to heaven with me when we die? I didn't like the answer I got.*

The next thing that happened was perhaps the most significant: Bailee began reassessing the pundits she had trusted and stepped outside her information silo. She read *AP* stories, listened to NPR, and following a wide range of thinkers on TikTok. As a result, she stopped following Shapiro, Walsh, Kelly, and Rogan.

I didn't realize how much I hadn't known. I only learned about the racist, bigoted, horrible things Trump had said once I changed my news sources.

Bailee had stepped outside the isolation of her subculture. Exposure to new ideas didn't cause her to change her views overnight—but it weakened the walls that had kept her from questioning anything at all.

Another crack in the MAGA wall came when the COVID-19 pandemic hit. Despite having greatly expanded her media diet, Bailee fell for one of the many conspiracy theories racing through MAGA, and shared it on Facebook. Someone reached out privately, explaining that the source wasn't credible and offering evidence to debunk it. *I felt so ashamed. So embarrassed.*

As the pandemic dragged on, Bailee watched Trump's daily COVID briefings and felt increasingly disturbed. *I kept hoping he'd get his act together, that he'd stop saying insane things—like telling people to inject bleach. But he never did.*

I entered a short-lived phase of identifying as a libertarian, and from that perspective, I thought Trump was the lesser of two evils compared with Joe Biden. Despite all my changes, I was still subject to manipulation. So I still voted for Trump in the 2020 election.

One Betrayal Too Many

January 6 changed everything. *There was no coming back from that. I could never support someone who instigated an attack on our democracy.* After a year of questioning, opening her mind to other perspectives and searching her heart, she fully severed her ties with Trump—and with MAGA.

Leaving MAGA didn't just change Bailee's politics. It changed her as a person. *It made me more empathetic. It allowed me to grow. Being in MAGA stunted me as a human being.*

Free from rigid ideology, Bailee began building her own belief system. She explored political frameworks like democratic socialism, which resonated deeply. She continued deconstructing her religious beliefs—and found herself moving further left than she ever imagined. *At this point, I'm probably further left than Bernie Sanders.*

Bailee's strong anti-abortion views changed after a conversation with her mother, who has serious health issues. *She told me that if she got pregnant at her age, she'd get an abortion, That broke my heart. Someone I love would have to make that choice.* That realization transformed her thinking. *I wanted my mother—and all women—to live.*

> Leaving MAGA...made me more empathetic. It allowed me to grow. Being in MAGA stunted me as a human being.

Her views on LGBTQ+ people changed too. *I didn't hate gay people, but I judged them. Now I understand that people can love who they love—and it doesn't harm me. It isn't sinful.*

Bailee voted for Democrats for the first time in the 2022 midterms and voted for Kamala Harris in 2024. She now lives in Tulsa and works with an organization defending public education from Oklahoma officials' efforts to undermine it.

Building a New Life—and a New Community

Finding the Leaving MAGA community helped Bailee heal. She greatly values the compassion, the openness, the willingness to listen. *I love the Leaving MAGA approach. The way we operate, people feel like they're not going to be judged, and that they can openly share their story. It made me feel like I wasn't alone, like other people had been where I was.*

As a former MAGA follower, I am sad and angry watching what Trump is doing in his second term. It's disheartening to hear the next horrible thing to come out of his mouth or show up on Truth Social. It's painful and exhausting. But I'm so glad I realized I was living in the MAGA echo chamber — and that I broke out of it!

And most of all, she's hopeful. *If I can change, others can too.*

For more of Bailee's story.

CHAPTER 13
Jay Gilley
Taking Back Control of My Life

There isn't one fix for this. It's going to take a multitude telling our stories.

Jay Gilley was born in 1988 in Mobile, Alabama. His mother withdrew him from public school in third grade to be homeschooled using an intensive religious curriculum. Jay found refuge in video games. It also helped him socially.

I had some friends, but they went to public schools, so there was a big cultural divide. I found common ground with them in gaming.

Jay's mother homeschooled him all the way through high school. His obsession with gaming continued into his twenties, and that's when he began his descent into extremism. *I was having a lot of trouble in the ladies' department, due in large part to not having a normal amount of socialization growing up. I fell down the rabbit hole of gamer anti-*

feminist videos and became a fan of the Incel and MGTOW (Men Going Their Own Way) movements.

He felt he had found a community; his fellow gamers were echoing his complaints about women. *I believed women were leading men on, lying about what they wanted from a man. ("You say you want a nice guy, but when a guy is nice you say you don't want that.") I believed that women only wanted "bad boys." I put all the blame for my romantic troubles on women; I never thought it was related to anything I was doing.*

Then the Gamergate controversy hit in 2014. *I agreed with a lot of the horrible things that were being posted about women. It all reinforced the stereotypes I was developing. That marked the beginning of my political life.*

Radicalized by White Nationalists

Jay also felt antipathy toward the Black Lives Matter movement. Growing up, his parents insisted that racism was a thing of the past, and that people who said it still existed were "crazy." He traces his anger toward Black Lives Matter to the protests that broke out after the 2014 killing of Michael Brown in Ferguson, Missouri.

I was one of those "all lives matter" people. I thought Black Lives Matter was racializing everything. In my mind, racism was over. We had solved it. We had a Black president. We weren't a racist country. My neighborhood was mixed, so that fed my perception that the country had moved past its racism.

To make matters worse, by the time of Ferguson, Jay had been radicalized by white nationalists, again through the gamer community. *They made comments on YouTube channels about how you can't make fun of any other race except White people. I was also influenced by the YouTuber Sargon of Akkad, who was very white nationalist.* (Sargon of Akkad is the pseudonym for British extremist Carl Benjamin, who played a key role in vilifying women in the Gamergate scandal.)

Looking back, Jay says he had no historical context for his beliefs. *My mom never taught us the history of racism, what Black Americans went through and still go through today. I was so ignorant; I had no understanding of how much prejudice and bias were baked into my belief system.*

President Barack Obama's support of Black Lives Matter fed Jay's distrust of the government. *I wondered, "Why are you helping racialize this?" I went down more social media rabbit holes, where I found those who said White people were the ones being discriminated against. I came to believe that society thought it was fine to talk about every other race's challenges, but not when it came to whites. My distrust of those pushing the narratives about racism grew. "Why are they pushing this?" I would ask myself. I came to feel like there was some sort of agenda.*

Coupled with his anti-feminism, Jay's racial outlook primed him to embrace MAGA.

Joining the MAGA Movement

Jay was also disappointed that Obama hadn't improved things for working people. Where he lived in Alabama, wages were stagnant, and having your own house or apartment, even affordable health care, seemed more and more out of reach. He thought nothing was ever going to get better, and that someone needed to shake the system up.

Then Trump started his first run for president. The first thing that caught my attention was when he said Mexico wasn't sending its best; it was sending its worst. He said some were rapists. In my mind, those were two different things; I didn't believe he was saying all Mexican immigrants were criminals. I felt people were lying about what he had said. I didn't understand that he was feeding people's biases.

Jay perked up when Trump called the mainstream media "fake news" and claimed they had an "agenda." *That played perfectly into my conspiracy theory that there was a hidden agenda about race.*

Jay didn't bother to vote in 2016 because he thought the system was rigged and Hillary Clinton was going to win. Trump's win totally shocked him. *I realized voting does work. I immediately got hooked on the anti-social justice warriors on YouTube: Ben Shapiro, Milo Yiannopoulos, and Steven Crowder, among others. I watched a lot of them and Tucker Carlson.*

I became very right-wing. I felt more and more that America was being attacked by a force from within. I totally bought into Trump's narrative of, "They're out to get you, and I'm the only thing standing in the way."

Though Jay did see things that seemed wrong, he found ways to defend, dismiss, or justify them. *Nothing that happened during Trump's first few years in office shook my support or made me question anything. If he did or said something controversial, I would just say, "Give him a chance."*

When Trump said there were "very fine people on both sides" after Charlottesville, I thought he wasn't talking about the neo-Nazis, but rather the folks who didn't want Confederate statues torn down for historical reasons.

> " *I became very right-wing. I felt more and more that America was being attacked by a force from within. I totally bought into Trump's narrative of, "They're out to get you, and I'm the only thing standing in the way."*

He was troubled by one thing: *I saw a lot of online communities I had been involved with become more anti-Semitic. People would say, "I'm not a Nazi, it's just that the Jews control everything." I thought that was insane thinking.*

Cracks in the MAGA Wall

A personal crisis jump-started Jay's journey out of MAGA. In trying to process his feelings about a woman, he suddenly saw a perspective besides his own. It would change everything.

In late 2018, the woman I had been involved with off and on for a bunch of years finally left me for good. I got very mad, and I was surrounded by people who told me I was right and she was wrong, that it was her fault, not mine.

In mid-2019, I was taking a walk, having an imaginary conversation with my ex in my head. I imagined her saying, "If I came back to you, but you knew I would never be happy, would you want me in your life?"

That hit me really hard; for the first time, I started thinking from her perspective. I had never taken her point of view into account. I tried to spend time outside my head and walk in her shoes. After two or three months of this, I came to empathize with what the feminist movement was saying back in 2014 during Gamergate. I couldn't believe what I had believed. That led me to have doubts about everything else. I thought, "I was wrong about this. What else was I wrong about?"

Jay did extensive research into Black Lives Matter, forcing himself to read articles and watch videos that challenged his views. *I spent a good six to nine months doing this. If I would get triggered or upset about the content, I would pause, walk away, and come back.*

I looked for people to talk to. I would go into the comments of the leftist content creators, learning how they thought about stuff. That community was very friendly, very open to me. I finally started to empathize with Black Lives Matter, realizing that my response to it had been ignorant.

One Betrayal Too Many

Jay continued to rationalize Trump's behavior for a time by telling himself the president was wrong on these issues because the people around him were misinforming him. Slowly but surely, he recognized the truth and started to turn away from MAGA.

When the pandemic hit, I took it very seriously as a public health threat. I couldn't believe Trump was downplaying it. I was already not entirely on board with him. When he started to pop off about how it was nothing, I thought, "This is a serious thing, you need to take this seriously. You're stupid or you're lying."

Then a Minneapolis police officer murdered George Floyd. In the aftermath, Jay saw a lot of disturbing videos. *I saw a lot of content across my feeds showing glaring differences in how people were treated by the cops. I saw White people being coddled, but if a Black person made the slightest wrong move their whole life was in danger. That was a huge wake-up call. Trump's hostility toward the Black Lives Matter protestors upset me. I thought, "You've got this entirely wrong, what are you doing?"*

By the fall of 2020, Jay was done with MAGA and Trump. *I stopped following Crowder, Carlson, Shapiro, and the rest. I turned to media I would never watch as a Trump/MAGA supporter: mainstream outlets like NBC and ABC. I felt I was getting caught up on a whole other world.*

I came to understand that Trump has no ability to be a leader, or to understand what's going on in the country. He has no interest in trying to lead or unite us. He has no interest in trying to understand what others are talking about. No true leader can be like that. I voted for Joe Biden in 2020.

Salvaging Lost Friendships

Jay's friends were angry when he left MAGA. He understood that they were stuck in the same mindset that had trapped him, but he tried to reason with them.

We argued a lot. I would say, "Just listen to me for a second." But they wouldn't; it was nonstop pushback. They were stuck in that toxic mindset and couldn't bring themselves to question the MAGA narrative at all. That was a very frustrating time.

He stopped talking to his friends for a few years. But then he decided to try again—a reminder to us all to be patient with one another. *I decided to reach out. I found old childhood photos on my computer and texted them, "Look what I found, you remember this?" We would reminisce and talk about things other than politics.*

By this point, Trump was president again. *Eventually they started raising concerns about what was going on. I just listened. They're angry about several things. They're mad that Trump did not follow through on his promise to lower the cost of living, and they're really mad that he fought so hard to prevent the Epstein files from being released. Now that they are getting released, my friends are upset that they're heavily redacted. "No innocent person would want them redacted," they say.*

Jay's friends are also angry about Trump's mass deportation campaign. *A number of them work in factories, so they're friends with a lot of Latinos, undocumented or otherwise. They were told the government was coming for the immigrants who were dangerous criminals, and now they see ICE targeting Home Depots and the law-abiding people they work with.*

They've seen the footage of ICE violently grabbing people off the streets. They see how it's spreading fear among their coworkers, including those who are here legally. They're all fearful, because it doesn't seem like ICE cares who it picks up. Seeing this fear in their coworkers really bothers them a lot.

He's encouraged to see his friends' views start to change. *I think at least some of them have started the long journey out of MAGA. Right now, they're falling back to the default line of, "All politicians are liars." That's just a deflection at this point, but I know the process takes time.*

Even my mom, who has been strongly MAGA for the past ten years, seems to have quietly left the movement. Trump angered her when he forced people to resume repaying their student loans, and she couldn't understand why he was trying to block the release of the Epstein files. We were talking about the upcoming governor's race in Alabama and my mom said she was looking at the Democratic candidates. She said she doesn't listen to Trump anymore.

Building a New Life—and a New Community

Jay now considers himself left or left-of-center. His main focus is trying to take as much accountability for his beliefs and actions as possible. *I can't just say, "Oh, I was lied to. It's my fault, because I let myself become that way."*

He is thankful to be free of the movement. *In MAGA, you spend all day, every day, in this state of paranoia and rage. Every little thing makes you outraged — and it's always everybody else's fault. You start getting fearful and paranoid of everybody who doesn't agree with you. It's so mentally taxing. Once I left, it was amazing how quickly that cloud lifted. It is also true that leaving is double-edged, because it made me fully aware of the gravity of our country's situation, and that has produced a lot of anxiety.*

Still, life now looks rosier to Jay. *Leaving the MAGA movement made me a better person. I got back control of my life. It's such an empowering feeling. For the first time in my life, I'm in a stable relationship. We've been together for four years, and our daughter is turning four this year. Walking away from MAGA gave me the opportunity to have a positive social life, to be a good romantic partner, and to be a good father.*

He's thankful to have found a community in Leaving MAGA. *For quite some time after I left MAGA, I felt I was alone. I didn't know of anyone else who had walked away. When I found out about Leaving MAGA, I felt called to talk to Rich and tell him my story, to let him know he's not alone either. Finding this organization was like finding a really good ally. Discovering that there were a lot of other people going through the exact same thing took a lot of the pressure off.*

Jay feels he has learned a lot from his fellow ex-MAGA members. *Getting to know the other people in Leaving MAGA has shown me there are any number of ways you can end up in the movement. That's been eye-opening. I've learned there isn't one way to fix this. It's going to take a multitude telling our stories. I also understand now that it's very important for anyone who's left MAGA to be as kind and open and honest as possible with those still in the movement.*

> For quite some time after I left MAGA, I felt I was alone. I didn't know of anyone else who had walked away. When I found out about Leaving MAGA, I felt called to talk to Rich and tell him my story, to let him know he's not alone either.

Leaving MAGA has given Jay new purpose. *Going public with my story felt so good mentally. Now I want to help people who are having doubts, are questioning, or are feeling lost. I want them to know it's okay to talk about it. I want to help them reach the point where they question how they believed this stuff in the first place, and to reflect—to ask themselves, "How did I get here?"*

For more of Jay's story.

CHAPTER 14

David Remington

Setting Down the Burden of Anger

It's so comforting to discover that I'm not the only one going through this.

David Remington was born in 1991 in Montana. His mom divorced his dad when he was six, and they moved to Portland. When David was twelve, his life abruptly changed when his mother passed away. His father relocated from Montana to Portland to raise him and his brother.

That transition began David's political journey. *My dad would always listen to conservative talk radio in the car— extreme stuff, like Michael Savage and Lars Larson. I fell hard for the narrative they were peddling. Even though I was only in middle school, I got heavily interested in politics. It became my whole world.*

David became very vocal about his right-wing politics, which did not go over well in liberal Portland. *I became a class troll. If I noticed my teachers saying something liberal or pressing the boundaries of politics, I would be combative. They were quite hostile toward my conservative views. Once a teacher put me in a time out for saying something extreme that I'd learned from talk radio.*

Whenever my beliefs were challenged, I would always push back. My philosophy was that you must always stand up for yourself and what you believe in, stand against the herd. I was really anti-gay, and even anti-disabled people. When the school had a special Day of Silence to honor LGBTQ+ kids, I declared it Loud and Proud Day. Because they knew where I stood on LGBTQ+ issues, sometimes my teachers would take me to another room when they were teaching a sex ed lesson. I would end up listening to conservative talk radio with the gym teacher.

David experienced a lot of harassment in middle school over his politics, so when he got to high school he chose to be less vocal. He felt alienated from his classmates and withdrew to the safety of online communities.

Being quiet about it made me cling to being conservative as something special. I didn't fit into the political culture in Portland. The internet was becoming a bigger thing around this time. I spent a lot of time online. I became more reclusive; to be honest, I became a bit of an internet addict. I connected with conservative online gamers.

Joining the MAGA Movement

After high school, David served in the Navy, then worked various jobs over the next several years while taking classes at Portland Community College. He studied everything from economics to art, which he loved. His politics hadn't changed, and when Donald Trump launched his first presidential campaign in 2015, David preferred him over the other Republican contenders.

His debate style was alluring to me, the way he defended himself, even talking over other candidates. As someone who felt standing up for your beliefs was the most important virtue you could have, I really admired how Trump stood up for his beliefs, even if it meant treating other people poorly.

I was a hardliner on immigration, so I liked Trump's approach to that issue. I believed that people who were illegally in the country had broken the law, so what was wrong with deporting them? It was just the law.

And I didn't see any harm in building a wall along the border. It made sense to me. I didn't have a problem with the comments Trump would make about migrants being murderers and rapists. I thought he was saying a truth people didn't want to admit.

I also supported Trump's energy policies. I was very anti-environmentalism. For a while, I was a climate change denier.

David became deeply immersed in MAGA. He also gravitated to more extremist movements. *I got into a lot of fringe politics. I followed Andy Ngo closely, right-wingers who posted on Twitter, and Trump. I fell into white identity politics, and I became a strong anti-feminist. Those positions stemmed more from a reaction against all things progressive. I didn't like the left, how people on the left treated me, how they went about their lives—I didn't like them as human beings.*

He did what he could to provoke his liberal adversaries. *I learned from a number of YouTubers how to inflame the other side when debating gender. I participated in one online controversy after another. I went to a couple of rallies organized by Patriot Prayer, but they got violent, so I stopped going. I went to a Build the Wall event at Washington State University. I waved a Trump flag, got my picture taken, and got in the news.*

David dismissed the controversy over the 2017 Unite the Right rally in Charlottesville. *I felt the whole thing was separate from the MAGA movement and Trump. When Trump said there were "very fine people on both sides," I thought it was a funny Trumpism. To me, it was another case of him saying something ridiculous and people going insane about it. I thought, "These Nazis exist, but what are you going to do about them?"*

Cracks in the MAGA Wall

After attending community college for several years, David enrolled at Portland State University in 2018. He majored in economics, with a minor in Judaic Studies. During his studies, he began to listen to other perspectives and found himself disagreeing with some MAGA policies.

It was an eye-opening experience; I discovered you could be an academic and be a Republican. I joined the College Republicans. I moved away from my fringe political beliefs, which felt good. Those of us in the College Republicans were Trump/MAGA supporters, but I scorned reactionary politics.

When the pandemic hit in 2020, David supported the president's approach. *I thought Trump was doing a really good job. He was first on the ball with the vaccine, which I got. I didn't think masks worked, although I now know I was wrong about that.*

Then came the 2020 election. *When Joe Biden defeated Trump, I didn't buy into Trump's claim that the election was stolen. I thought, "This is over. It sucks that he lost, but I'm going to go on to live my life."*

One Betrayal Too Many

David's break with MAGA began with the January 6 attack on the Capitol.

It was shocking, especially because Trump was behind it. As a veteran, I would never commit sedition or take up arms against the government. Trump and his supporters tried to say January 6 was like the riots in Portland after George Floyd was killed. But I thought that was clearly a false equivalency.

I largely turned away from politics and focused on my art, but I still stuck with MAGA. At the same time, my doubts were growing. I was learning a lot in college and was seeing that some of Trump's arguments didn't make any sense.

> **"** *(January 6) was shocking, especially because Trump was behind it. As a veteran, I would never commit sedition or take up arms against the government.*

For example, I took a climate ethics class. It was illuminating; it gave credence to the scientific orthodoxy about climate change. The class made me feel like I was being foolish to think I knew the science better than the experts. I was so thankful I went to college and discovered the right-wing scare stories about professors teaching malicious stuff weren't true. They were just teaching us facts.

During Biden's time in office, David continued searching for less conservative perspectives and realized the disconnect between how he wanted to live his life and MAGA politics.

I realized there was so much misinformation in the world. I started watching CNN, listening to NPR, and reading The Guardian. I was content during Biden's presidency. We didn't have big controversies, the country was stable, you could do what you wanted.

Focusing so much on my art was another factor that helped me eventually leave MAGA. The artistic aesthetic is empathetic and forgiving. Those traits are a central part of my being. As a result, I recognized the mismatch with my politics, which were quite cruel.

The disconnect became even clearer when Trump jumped into the 2024 presidential race. *Trump's energy policy didn't make any sense, nor did his economic policies. The very notion of America First seemed in many ways to actually mean America Alone. And he was making a lot of ridiculous remarks, like claiming Haitian immigrants were eating cats and dogs.*

I found MAGA's treatment of Republicans who angered Trump in one way or another offensive. For example, calling Mike Pence a traitor. How is he a traitor? All he did was stand up for the Constitution.

The closest thing to a "come to Jesus" moment for me occurred when Trump boycotted the Republican primary debates. For one thing, they were so civil without him in the room. And it showed he didn't give a shit about the party; it was a grave insult to conservatives.

Building a New Life—and a New Community

David was done with MAGA. He became more open to the Democratic Party and its ideas and even voted for Kamala Harris. Now that Trump is president again, he feels vindicated in his beliefs about him and is open about how his views have evolved.

He's wrecking the country. Look at all the financial instability he's created with his tariffs, which are completely against the American economy and our well-being. Trump's slashing jobs at the VA is really offensive. Some of the people in charge of my health care are under attack. His immigration policy is awful.

As part of my political evolution, I've become very open to immigrants, now that I understand the huge economic and social contributions they make to this country. I take great offense when people in MAGA say immigrants who come to the US and become *successful aren't legitimate Americans, because they're not "Heritage Americans." My heritage dates back to the Mayflower, but it's totally backward to say someone doesn't belong here if they aren't a Heritage American. I mean, there are only a few million of us with that type of*

> **The very notion of America First seemed in many ways to actually mean America Alone.**

lineage, and in this nation of immigrants, we need immigrants more than anything.

David also experienced a turnaround on cultural issues; he is now supportive of LGBTQ+ people. *I'm upset about Trump's attacks against the trans community. I have been reading the Bible a lot more since the election. A main point of the Bible is that those without sin shall cast the first stone. But that part of the Bible is totally missing from how people are treating trans people. For example, Andy Ngo, a guy I used to like and give money to, now says trans people are the real terrorists. That seems inhuman; at least treat them like human beings.*

He is also alarmed by Trump's assault on the Constitution. *I have always considered myself a conservative Republican, but when Trump took office this time around and started issuing so many anti-democratic executive orders, I realized that our essential liberties are under threat—and that I had taken those liberties for granted. Now I consider myself a libertarian—not an anarcho-capitalist, but a believer in maximum liberty, Milton Friedman-style.*

I see MAGA as a movement that turned against what I grew up believing. It's against the military, it's against good economic policy, and it's against a lot of conservative values.

David understands how difficult it is to leave a community behind, but he recognizes what a difference walking away from MAGA has made in his life. *It was unsettling to leave MAGA. I initially felt a big loss of security. Instead of enjoying the camaraderie of my fellow members of the movement, suddenly I was the enemy. When you walk away, you're setting foot onto unexplored territory, and while that's exciting, it's also scary.*

He regrets the role he played in bringing Trump to power and feels compelled to speak out. *It's all so awful, and I helped bring it about. That's why it's so important for me to go public, to tell the world that MAGA is based on a foundation of lies, fear, and hatred, and that Donald Trump is undermining our very democracy.*

It's not easy [speaking publicly] because many of my friends are still in MAGA. Sometimes I feel like I'm betraying them, but in the end, I know that's not true. I'm fighting for them.

David wants people to know how liberating it feels to quit the movement. *I want people to understand that being in MAGA is a mental prison. You dehumanize those who disagree with you. You feel you can only be friends with others in MAGA. You consider people on the left to be terrorists, crazy, all sorts of outrageous things. It's a great feeling leaving that mental prison.*

I'm not angry all the time anymore. It takes a lot of energy to be angry and hateful every day. It's a big burden, and removing that burden has been a life-changer. Studying in college has helped me tremendously as well. It has made me less dogmatic and less judgmental of others.

On top of meeting new friends, leaving MAGA has opened other doors for me too. I have been making more friends who are left-wing. I used to write them off as dangerous; now I see them as comprehensive, interesting people. Taking this step has changed my perspective on the world for the better.

David is grateful to have found the Leaving MAGA organization, because it has given him a way to connect with others who, like himself, have chosen to leave MAGA behind. *Finding the Leaving MAGA community has been wonderful. It's so comforting to discover that there are other people like me, that I'm not the only one going through this.* **For more of David's story.**

C H A P T E R 15
Jennie Gage

From Religious Trauma to Freedom of Thought

I'm trying to write a better future for my kids, and yours.

Jennie Gage was born in 1974 in Medford, Oregon, into a family with Mormon roots stretching back to her great-grandparents. *We were a very traditional, very old-fashioned Mormon family, so mom stayed at home to raise the kids. The church dominated our lives: religious study at home Monday nights, youth group Wednesday nights, Saturday potlucks, and church all day on Sundays.*

When she was about seven, her school tested Jennie and determined she was gifted. *They pulled me out of school two days a week to bus me to another school that had a program for gifted kids. I loved it; we were doing amazing stuff, in particular learning critical thinking and problem-solving. I felt like my brain was being tickled.*

Unfortunately, after I finished fifth grade my dad decided to move from our home in Oregon to go to school in

Scottsdale, Arizona, and there was no gifted program there. But those critical thinking skills would come in handy later.

Pre-MAGA Influences

Jennie's Mormon upbringing hammered home the church's thinking about women's role in society. *I started in the Mormon church's young women's program when I was twelve. It's designed to prepare you for trad wife life. They taught us how to take care of kids, how to cook, how to scrub a toilet, how to be a good conversationalist (so we could be good wives), and how to iron a man's shirt. It was depressing.*

When she graduated from high school in 1992, Jennie didn't want to be a traditional Mormon wife and mom. *I enrolled at Ricks College (now BYU Idaho) in Rexburg, Idaho. Now, Mormon girls aren't supposed to go to college to learn; you go to find a husband. But I dreamed of becoming a Russian-speaking international trade attorney.*

Before classes started, my counselor told me I could keep Russian, but I had to drop pre-law so I could take classes on dating and marriage. In the end, I ended up following the trajectory the counselor had laid out for me.

Within two months of starting college, at the age of eighteen, Jennie got engaged to someone she deeply loved. But she put their marriage plans on hold while he completed his two-year Mormon mission. Jennie went on to get an AA in Russian with a minor in political science. Before her fiancé returned, a church leader persuaded Jennie to go on a date with a returning missionary. He said the Holy Ghost told him that "Jake" was her future husband.

I was raised to believe the Holy Ghost spoke to people, so I reluctantly agreed to meet Jake. On our second date, he molested me. Jake felt bad about it, so we went to confess to the bishop. When Jake told him what he'd done, the bishop said, "We need to hurry up and get you guys married." The wedding was six weeks later. I married a stranger who had molested me.

Marriage was a nightmare; Jake started physically abusing me within a week of our wedding. I wanted to get a divorce, but everyone said I couldn't because we'd been married in a Mormon temple. My nightmare lasted twenty-four years. I was regularly abused and constantly wanted to die; I had anxiety and depression.

During those twenty-four years, Jennie and her husband were quite well off, owning businesses, building a home, vacationing in Hawaii, and driving Mercedes and BMWs. Politically, they were very conservative.

As good Mormons, we were waiting for Jesus to come back any day. I didn't think I'd live long enough to have grandkids. White supremacy was baked into our belief system. The Book of Mormon says white people are better, and dark-skinned people are cursed. We were anti-abortion and we thought homosexuality was the most evil thing in the world. I spent a lot of time and money helping fight Proposition 8 (which would have legalized same-sex marriage) in California.

We listened to Rush Limbaugh all the time—never missed an episode. I listened to Glenn Beck quite a bit. I watched Fox News when it came along. I never watched the mainstream networks or CNN.

Jennie didn't have a lot of time to think about politics. *Mostly I was busy keeping my house clean, raising babies and chickens, keeping my hair and nails perfect, and cooking every meal from scratch.*

She began having major health issues in 2011, when she was thirty-six. Complications from surgery to remove a benign ovarian tumor nearly killed her. *We had never bothered to get health insurance, so I wasn't able to get some of the care I needed. I was in and out of the hospital for years…we ended up in medical bankruptcy.* Meanwhile, Jake's abuse intensified.

While Jennie was recovering, they moved to a small town in South Carolina. *It was there that I got radicalized into Christian fundamentalism and a more extreme form of racism. Our neighbors were "normal" people: they lived in beautiful homes, tended their farms, raised their horses. They went to church on Sundays, had big happy families with cute little housewives and successful dads. And many of them belonged to the Ku Klux Klan. We were invited to join but didn't, because Mormons don't believe in joining other groups and are nonviolent. I did become a sympathizer, though. I was an easy target, since I believed Heavenly Father had chosen white people to be smarter and better than Black people, who were vicious and animalistic.*

Joining the MAGA Movement

By this point, Donald Trump was running for president the first time, and Jennie enthusiastically supported him. *I was already a longtime fan; I had fallen in love with Trump watching The Apprentice. I never missed an episode. I was obsessed with his whole persona. I had The Art of the Deal and The Art of the Comeback. I underlined passages and wrote notes in the margins. I felt euphoric that America had the possibility to have this incredibly smart businessman running our country.*

My Mormonism prepared me to embrace Trump and MAGA. We were taught that God made America as a promised land for his most righteous children. Christian Nationalism was a natural outgrowth of my religion. We mixed America with the Gospel; I believed the Constitution was written by God, and that the national anthem and "God Bless America" were religious songs.

MAGA became my whole identity. Trump was my personal profile picture on social media. I posted love letters to him. Trump used rhetoric that persuaded me that he had converted to Christianity. It was so impressive to me that this rich New York playboy who'd spent his younger days carousing had now found Jesus. Now he was a family man who was called by God to lead the country.

Trump's hate resonated with me too. He hated lesbians, gay people, trans people, foreigners. Every Sunday in church we were taught that half of humanity was going to burn in hell, and Trump really played into that. So, whenever he said something hateful, I really enjoyed it. Here was

> "My Mormonism prepared me to embrace Trump and MAGA. We were taught that God made America as a promised land for his most righteous children. Christian Nationalism was a natural outgrowth of my religion.

someone who as president was going to call out the people who were evil.

When Trump won the 2016 election, Jennie believed the country was entering a Camelot-style era. She looked forward to a return to family values, a strong economy, more money and more peace.

I routinely promoted Trump on my social media platforms. I decided to only hang out with Trump supporters. I felt Trump was running the country like the Mormon prophet was running the church. My religious community was a dictatorship, so I wasn't used to democracy. In fact, I questioned why we needed it. In the church, if the prophet is inspired, he just changes a policy. Once Trump said he owned a copy of the Book of Mormon. Rumors spread throughout our community that he had read it. I prayed every day that he would convert.

Trump's authoritarian streak, his banning people from the country, his claim that there were "fine people on both sides" after Charlottesville, that all really resonated with me. Remember, I lived in a religious community that was always banning everything. I wasn't allowed to watch certain movies, listen to certain music, or even wear my own underwear.

Cracks in the MAGA Wall

As Jake's abuse escalated, Jennie separated from him for a time, then returned in the hope of reconciling. *I hoped Jesus had done His job and changed my husband's heart. But he was as abusive as ever.* Jennie didn't know it, but her life was about to change dramatically.

On October 7, 2018, I went to church, really stressed out—and something snapped in me. Those critical thinking skills I'd learned as a kid took over. The first hour was dedicated to telling us women aren't supposed to work. I looked around at the working women in the congregation, including a doctor and a schoolteacher. The judgment and hatred in those remarks hit me hard.

Then several dozen of the women spent an hour in Sunday school. The preacher said the Holocaust happened because the Jews killed Jesus. I couldn't believe everyone sat there unquestioningly. The third hour's lesson focused on the evils of homosexuality. I thought of lesbian friends I had made in a previous business venture, of a gay cousin my family had shunned. All of a sudden, I connected the dots. My hands were shaking. It was almost like an out-of-body experience.

I thought to myself, I come to church to learn how to love people better, not to learn how to hate. But the church had preached hate my whole life. I raised my hand, I stood up, grabbed my purse and keys, and announced I was leaving the church because of the lesson.

Jennie and Jake left the Mormon church and started attending a Christian church that, at the time, felt wonderful and healing. A few weeks later, however, she ended their marriage after catching Jake with a prostitute. He cleaned out their bank account and threatened to take their kids. Jennie was devastated.

I had lost my faith in God, my belief in everything. In early December 2018, I tried to kill myself through carbon monoxide poisoning. Two of my kids still lived at home, but they were at school. Thankfully, a neighbor heard my car running and rescued me. After ten days in a coma, I survived.

I decided that I had to deconstruct everything I had believed in and build a new life for myself. I questioned what I believed about the Bible, about Jesus, about marriage and gender roles. That began my journey out of MAGA, but trying to survive pushed politics to the side.

Starting in late 2019, after Jake canceled the lease on her home, Jennie spent three months homeless. Finally, an aunt and uncle let her and her children move into their abandoned guest house outside of Tucson that they were repairing. *It was in the middle of the desert, with javelinas and rattlesnakes as our nearest neighbors. Things were still very rough. I was having seizures—a side effect of carbon monoxide poisoning. Then the pandemic hit, and I almost died from COVID.*

One Betrayal Too Many

During this difficult time, Jennie's boyfriend moved to Tucson to help care for her. After a commitment ceremony and the blending of their families, she began to publish TikTok videos about leaving the Mormon church. Jennie's followers (now a half million strong) provided community and an appreciation that there was life after leaving the church. It was then that her journey out of MAGA accelerated.

I read books on racism, feminism, and gender. I listened to podcasts. I befriended other creators, authors, and influencers, many of them very liberal. I was getting the education I'd never had. Everyone was very patient with me, particularly as I unraveled and rejected the racism that had defined me.

My previous worldview collapsed. I realized most of what I'd believed wasn't true. I completed my journey out of MAGA once the 2024 campaign got going. After everything I had learned, I was still willing to give Trump one more chance. I think I wanted to cling to something from my old life that I thought made sense. But as I watched Trump at his rallies, I heard the same hatred I heard in the Mormon church and in my Christian church. It struck me that he sounded like my narcissistic ex-husband.

I realized I didn't actually know what the Democratic and Republican parties stood for. I studied each party's platform and positions and discovered I didn't believe in anything the Republicans were supporting. I found myself agreeing with the Democrats' positions.

Building a New Life—and a New Community

Jennie is thankful she left MAGA, and enjoys sharing her story. *Sometimes I feel I'm having an out-of-body experience, because I'm such a dramatically different person. I am empathetic to the point that sometimes it's painful. Instead of feeling hateful and afraid all the time, I now try to live my life in harmony with others, in peace. I'm much more positive in general about the world, so much so that I'm almost delusional! My mantra is, "We're going to be okay." I'm enjoying the ride of life.*

I'm trying to build a life based on common sense, compassion, and empathy. I'm working hard to push back against everything I once stood for and change the world. It's the least I can do. I read somewhere that today we are writing the future our kids will act out tomorrow. I'm trying to write a better future for my kids, and yours. They deserve it.

I have started to build a community of people from all over the country who are ex-MAGA, ex-Mormon, ex-evangelical, ex-Catholic. I've become a women's rights activist, especially around domestic violence. I work with a national organization that helps survivors. I volunteer with Secular Arizona and attend school board meetings.

> "I'm trying to build a life based on common sense, compassion, and empathy. I'm working hard to push back against everything I once stood for and change the world. It's the least I can do.

Before I discovered Leaving MAGA, I thought I was a lone wolf, the only one who had left the movement. When Rich Logis first reached out to tell me about the organization, it felt like someone wrapped me up in this warm blanket and said, "Jennie, you can breathe now." It was so comforting.

Finding others who have left MAGA has been cathartic and healing. It gives me hope for the world, like people are waking up. I love watching the short videos of my Leaving MAGA partners. They're very inspiring; I watch them and I'm spurred to share them far and wide. I imagine those of us in Leaving MAGA standing together, holding our arms out to those who are questioning their fealty to Trump.

For more of Jennie's story.

CONCLUSION

I hope this book has given insight into how people fall into MAGA, and how there are many different paths that can lead to that destination. I also hope you have learned that, despite people's seemingly intractable support for Donald Trump, it is possible to find one's way out of MAGA.

I know there are many MAGA Americans, perhaps millions, who are experiencing doubts or asking questions about whether they've been lied to. Perhaps those questions have arisen because of the brutality and lawlessness of the deportation campaign. Perhaps it was the attempted coverup of the Epstein files, the pursuit of foreign wars, or the failure to improve the economy. Some are outraged that Trump shared racist images of a former president.

Whatever the reason or reasons, my job—and I hope you will join me in this endeavor—is to greet those who are casting their eyes beyond the walls of the MAGA echo chamber with empathy and compassion. I completely understand the anger of those who feel people who are only now questioning their loyalty to MAGA don't deserve those things, that they should have seen the light years ago. But our very democracy is at stake, and scorn and derision will not win new recruits to the cause of saving our republic.

My journey, and those of the others who have joined Leaving MAGA, prove that providing a welcoming, non-judgmental off-ramp is the best way to encourage people to walk away from Trump

As I said in my introduction to this book, I formed Leaving MAGA to provide those who are having doubts about their continued involvement with MAGA a space for healing and the freedom to discover their own path. You don't have to become a card-carrying Democrat if you leave MAGA. You don't have to compromise your morals. Remember, the Leaving MAGA community is made up of conservatives, moderates, and progressives.

You don't have to agree with my politics to recognize that Donald Trump and MAGA have betrayed fundamental American values. He is shredding the Constitution, weaponizing the government against his enemies, and corruptly enriching himself and his family, all while ignoring average Americans' needs.

We also need the friends and family of those who have left MAGA to do their part. Welcome your loved ones with open arms. Work with humility to create healing and reconciliation.

And if you have a friend or relative in MAGA who has removed a brick or two from the wall, please share this book with them. It could be the lifeline they need.

ACKNOWLEDGMENTS

This book would not exist without those who have stood with me, first as I left MAGA, then as I launched the Leaving MAGA organization, and now with the writing of *One Betrayal Too Many*.

I am grateful to Dr. Carl Procario-Foley, who has served as a mentor since my college days, and who offered critical support as I struggled with leaving MAGA.

I also want to express my gratitude to the people who supported me during the journey of creating Leaving MAGA. There are too many to name, but I do want to mention those who were with me at the beginning: Adam Kinzinger, Paul Glickman, Nadine Smith, Lia Gaines, Christopher Deutsch, and Keith Knueven. I could never have accomplished this without you.

Leaving MAGA is blessed to have a stellar team of volunteers and staff, who breathe life into our mission and lead our growth. You all have my deepest gratitude:

- John Bates, Public Speaking Coach
- Julianna Forlano, Support Group Facilitator
- Shannon Giovannone, Social Media Director
- Paul Glickman, Editorial Director
- Ray Tarara, Co-Chief Videographer
- Joey Vaughan, Co-Chief Videographer

A huge thank you to Noelle Cook, Zach Elwood, and Brandon Freeny, Leaving MAGA's founding board members. Your commitment to our mission strengthens our community and helps create a welcoming space for those who leave MAGA.

To all those who let Leaving MAGA share your stories on our website, I am deeply grateful. A special thank you to those whose testimonials are included in this book: Jennie Gage, Jay Gilley, Stephania Messina, David Remington, Bailee Tyler, and Steve Vilchez. Thank you to the rest of our Leaving MAGA leaders: Anthony Brooks, K.C. Cain, Danny Collins, Charles Ekokotu, Steven Francisci, PattyAnn Giles, James Hicks, Victoria Hurst, Jerry Koch, Madison Morrison, Deanna Raper, Jason Riddle, Erica Roach, Courtney Rosenberg, Michael Sirback, and Justin Yu. And thank you to all those who will be adding their names to this list.

Finally, I want to thank the wonderful folks at my publisher, Writers Integrity Network (WIN), who approached me with the idea of writing this book and then collaborated closely with me in its creation: Carolyn Rafferty, Publisher; Carmen Berry, Editorial Director; and Kay McConnaughey, for a brilliant cover design. An extra acknowledgment goes to Paul Glickman, who offered significant editorial assistance. Together, we have been a winning team.

ABOUT RICH LOGIS

Rich Logis is the founder and CEO of Leaving MAGA. He has dedicated his life to undoing the political damage he caused during his seven years as a devoted MAGA activist, pundit and podcaster. He is especially proud of the growing number of testimonials Leaving MAGA has published of others who have left MAGA, and of the organization's support group for people with friends and family in the movement. Rich has a large social media following, frequently speaks around the country, and has been featured on CNN, MS NOW, and many other outlets, including major foreign newspapers and TV programs. He lives in Florida with his wife and two daughters. When he's not empowering people to leave MAGA, Rich catches up on reading, spends time with his family and roots for the Boston Celtics.

For more information about Leaving MAGA.

ABOUT THE PUBLISHER
Writers Integrity Network

www.writersintegritynetwork.com

Writers Integrity Network (WIN) is a new pro-democracy publishing house that mobilizes writers whose books unite and equip Americans to confront the current assault on American democracy.

Editorial Director / Carmen Renee Berry is a *New York Times* bestselling author whose publishers include HarperCollins, Simon & Schuster, Penguin, and Thomas Nelson. Over the past forty years, she has authored, coauthored, and ghostwritten over forty books, selling over a million and a half copies and translated into nine languages. She holds a Master's in Social Work.
Contact: carmen@writersintegritynetwork.com

Publisher / Carolyn Rafferty has over forty years of experience in professional media production and distribution. Her newest publishing venture is the formation of the Writers Integrity Network. She holds a Master's Degree in Intercultural Studies
Contact: carolyn@writersintegritynetwork.com

For more information about Writers Integrity Network.